SCHOLASTIC

ALPHA Grammar and Composition 4

Anne Seaton
Series editor: Anne Seaton

About ALPHA™ Grammar and Composition

Welcome to **Scholastic ALPHA™ Grammar and Composition.**

This series comprises coursebooks for classes 1 to 5 and offers an easy, engaging and meaningful way to master the skills and mechanics of English **Grammar**, **Composition** and **Comprehension**.

Easy recall of prior topic followed by an exercise to check for readiness to learn

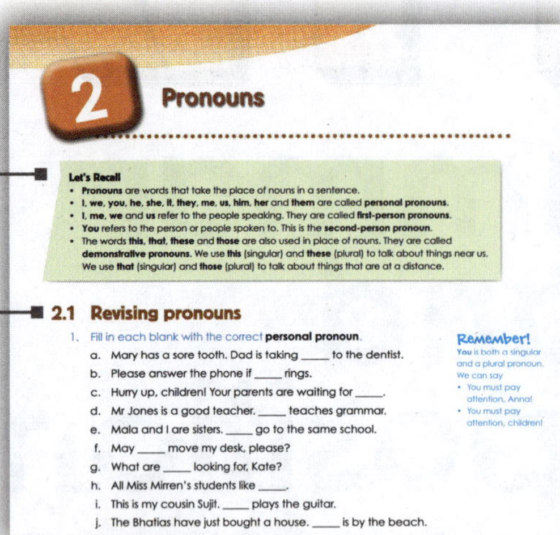

2 Pronouns

Let's Recall

- **Pronouns** are words that take the place of nouns in a sentence.
- **I, we, you, he, she, it, they, me, us, him, her** and **them** are called **personal pronouns**.
- **I, me, we** and **us** refer to the people speaking. They are called **first-person pronouns**.
- **You** refers to the person or people spoken to. This is the **second-person pronoun**.
- The words **this, that, these** and **those** are also used in place of nouns. They are called **demonstrative pronouns**. We use **this** (singular) and **these** (plural) to talk about things near us. We use **that** (singular) and **those** (plural) to talk about things that are at a distance.

2.1 Revising pronouns

1. Fill in each blank with the correct **personal pronoun**.
   a. Mary has a sore tooth. Dad is taking ____ to the dentist.
   b. Please answer the phone if ____ rings.
   c. Hurry up, children! Your parents are waiting for ____.
   d. Mr Jones is a good teacher. ____ teaches grammar.
   e. Mala and I are sisters. ____ go to the same school.
   f. May ____ move my desk, please?
   g. What are ____ looking for, Kate?
   h. All Miss Mirren's students like ____.
   i. This is my cousin Sujit. ____ plays the guitar.
   j. The Bhatias have just bought a house. ____ is by the beach.

Grammar focus through an engaging picture story

Related exercises for meaningful learning

Simple definition to explain each grammar concept

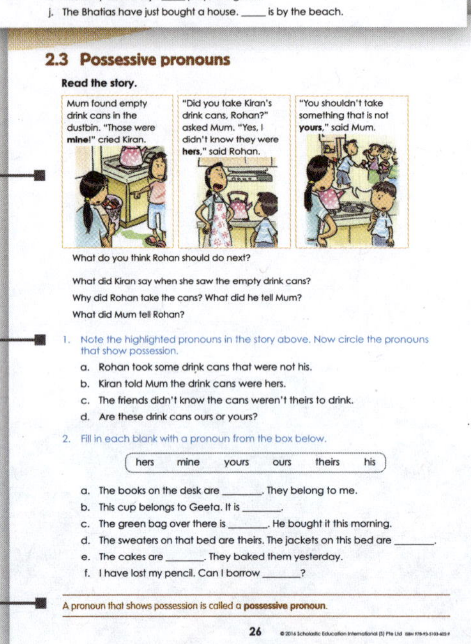

2.3 Possessive pronouns

Read the story.

What do you think Rohan should do next?

What did Kiran say when she saw the empty drink cans?
Why did Rohan take the cans? What did he tell Mum?
What did Mum tell Rohan?

1. Note the highlighted pronouns in the story above. Now circle the pronouns that show possession.
   a. Rohan took some drink cans that were not his.
   b. Kiran told Mum the drink cans were hers.
   c. The friends didn't know the cans weren't theirs to drink.
   d. Are these drink cans ours or yours?
2. Fill in each blank with a pronoun from the box below.

   hers mine yours ours theirs his

   a. The books on the desk are ______. They belong to me.
   b. This cup belongs to Geeta. It is ______.
   c. The green bag over there is ______. He bought it this morning.
   d. The sweaters on that bed are theirs. The jackets on this bed are ______.
   e. The cakes are ______. They baked them yesterday.
   f. I have lost my pencil. Can I borrow ______?

A pronoun that shows possession is called a **possessive pronoun**.

26

Practice exercises for meaningful application of the concept

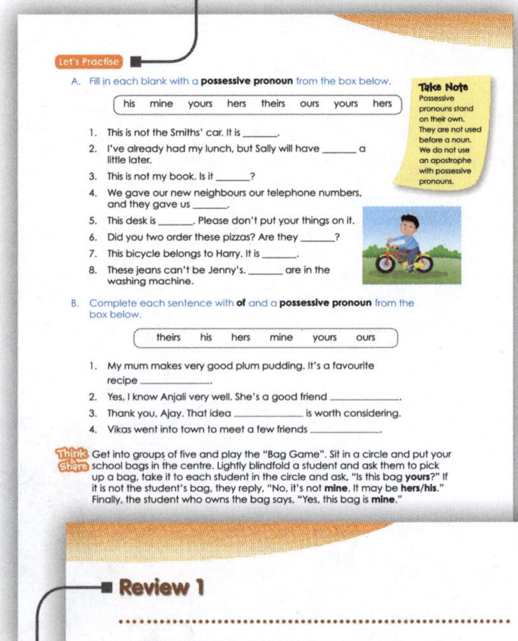

Let's Practise

A. Fill in each blank with a **possessive pronoun** from the box below.

   his mine yours hers theirs ours yours hers

   1. This is not the Smiths' car. It is ______.
   2. I've already had my lunch, but Sally will have ______ a little later.
   3. This is not my book. Is it ______?
   4. We gave our new neighbours our telephone numbers, and they gave us ______.
   5. This desk is ______. Please don't put your things on it.
   6. Did you two order these pizzas? Are they ______?
   7. This bicycle belongs to Harry. It is ______.
   8. These jeans can't be Jenny's. ______ are in the washing machine.

Take Note Possessive pronouns stand on their own. They are not used before a noun. We do not use an apostrophe with possessive pronouns.

B. Complete each sentence with **of** and a **possessive pronoun** from the box below.

   theirs his hers mine yours ours

   1. My mum makes very good plum pudding. It's a favourite recipe ______.
   2. Yes, I know Anjali very well. She's a good friend ______.
   3. Thank you, Ajay. That idea ______ is worth considering.
   4. Vikas went into town to meet a few friends ______.

Think & Share Get into groups of five and play the "Bag Game". Sit in a circle and put your school bags in the centre. Lightly blindfold a student and ask them to pick up a bag, take it to each student in the circle and ask, "Is this bag **yours**?" If it is not the student's bag, they reply, "No, it's not **mine**. It may be **hers/his**." Finally, the student who owns the bag says, "Yes, this bag is **mine**."

Periodic reviews to consolidate learning and for systematic assessment

Spot the Error to provide an opportunity for error correction

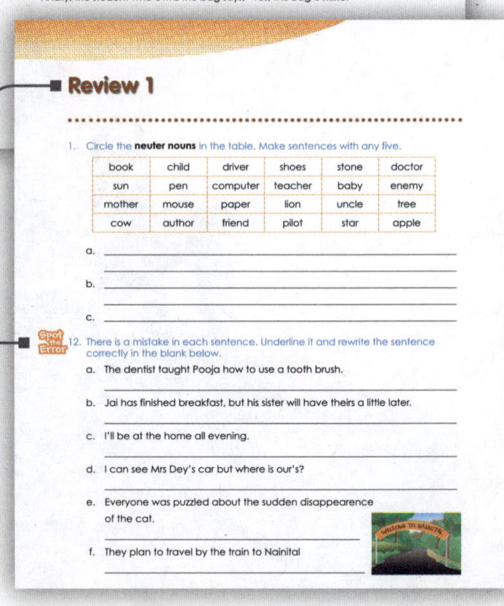

Review 1

1. Circle the **neuter nouns** in the table. Make sentences with any five.

book	child	driver	shoes	stone	doctor
sun	pen	computer	teacher	baby	enemy
mother	mouse	paper	lion	uncle	tree
cow	author	friend	pilot	star	apple

a.
b.
c.

Spot the Error 12. There is a mistake in each sentence. Underline it and rewrite the sentence correctly in the blank below.

a. The dentist taught Pooja how to use a tooth brush.
b. Jai has finished breakfast, but his sister will have theirs a little later.
c. I'll be at the home all evening.
d. I can see Mrs Dey's car but where is our's?
e. Everyone was puzzled about the sudden disappearence of the cat.
f. They plan to travel by the train to Nainital

- **Take Note** provides additional tips and exceptions to rules.
- **Think & Share** activities allow opportunity for collaborative learning.
- **Remember** enhances the understanding of the concept being taught in the unit.

 ISBN 978-93-5103-602-9

Graded exercises develop key comprehension and critical thinking skills

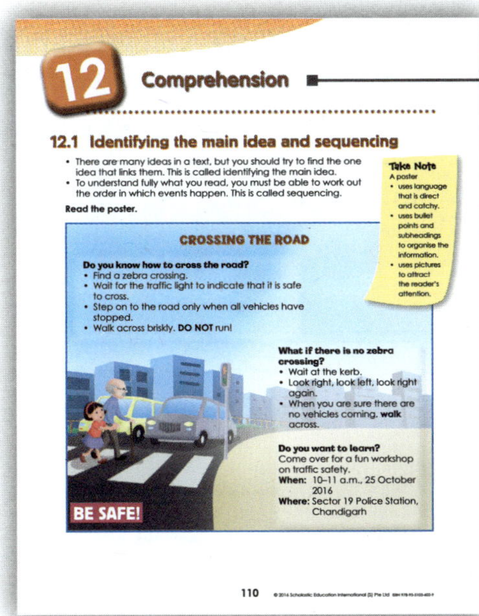

12 Comprehension

12.1 Identifying the main idea and sequencing

- There are many ideas in a text, but you should try to find the one idea that links them. This is called identifying the main idea.
- To understand fully what you read, you must be able to work out the order in which events happen. This is called sequencing.

Read the poster.

Take Note
A poster
- uses language that is direct and catchy.
- uses bullet points and subheadings to organise the information.
- uses pictures to attract the reader's attention.

110

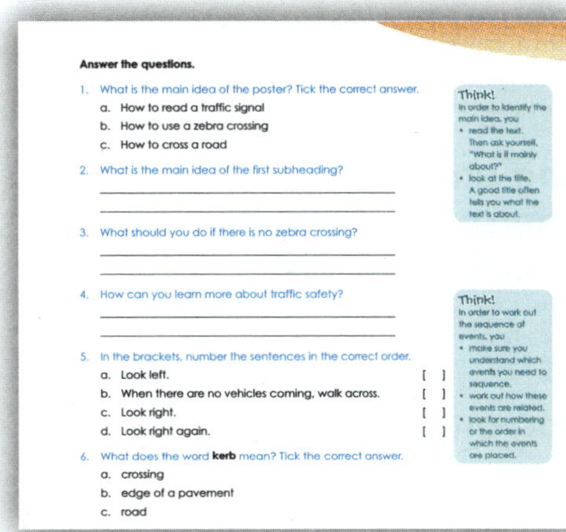

Answer the questions.

1. What is the main idea of the poster? Tick the correct answer.
   a. How to read a traffic signal
   b. How to use a zebra crossing
   c. How to cross a road
2. What is the main idea of the first subheading?
   ____
   ____
3. What should you do if there is no zebra crossing?
   ____
   ____
4. How can you learn more about traffic safety?
   ____
   ____
5. In the brackets, number the sentences in the correct order.
   a. Look left. [ ]
   b. When there are no vehicles coming, walk across. [ ]
   c. Look right. [ ]
   d. Look right again. [ ]
6. What does the word **kerb** mean? Tick the correct answer.
   a. crossing
   b. edge of a pavement
   c. road

Think!
In order to identify the main idea, you
- read the text. Then ask yourself, "What is it mainly about?"
- look at the title. A good title often tells you what the text is about.

Think!
In order to work out the sequence of events, you
- make sure you understand which events you need to sequence.
- work out how these events are related.
- look for numbering or the order in which the events are placed.

Scaffolded exercises to develop key writing skills across varied genres and topics

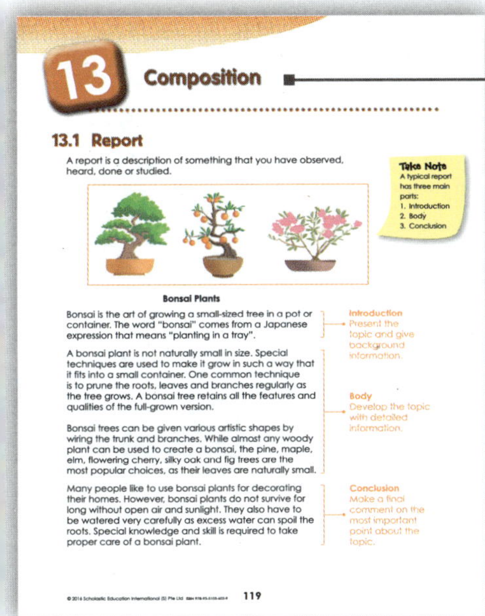

13 Composition

13.1 Report

A report is a description of something that you have observed, heard, done or studied.

Take Note
A typical report has three main parts:
1. Introduction
2. Body
3. Conclusion

Bonsai Plants

Bonsai is the art of growing a small-sized tree in a pot or container. The word "bonsai" comes from a Japanese expression that means "planting in a tray".

Introduction Present the topic and give background information.

A bonsai plant is not naturally small in size. Special techniques are used to make it grow in such a way that it fits into a small container. One common technique is to prune the roots, leaves and branches regularly as the tree grows. A bonsai tree retains all the features and qualities of the full-grown version.

Bonsai trees can be given various artistic shapes by wiring the trunk and branches. While almost any woody plant can be used to create a bonsai, the pine, maple, elm, flowering cherry, silky oak and fig trees are the most popular choices, as their leaves are naturally small.

Body Develop the topic with detailed information.

Many people like to use bonsai plants for decorating their homes. However, bonsai plants do not survive for long without open air and sunlight. They also have to be watered very carefully as excess water can spoil the roots. Special knowledge and skill is required to take proper care of a bonsai plant.

Conclusion Make a final comment on the most important point about the topic.

119

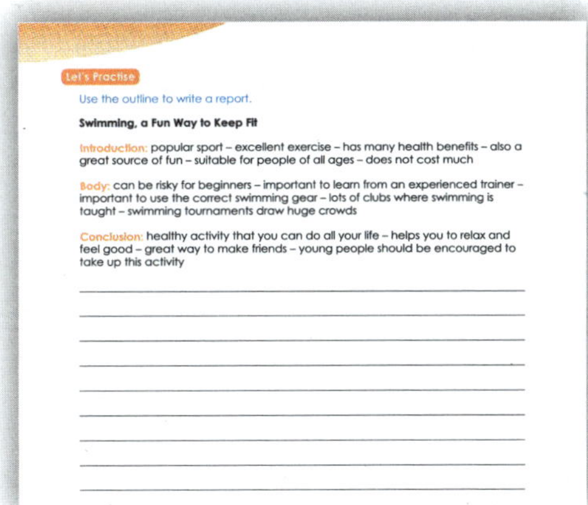

Let's Practise

Use the outline to write a report.

Swimming, a Fun Way to Keep Fit

Introduction: popular sport – excellent exercise – has many health benefits – also a great source of fun – suitable for people of all ages – does not cost much

Body: can be risky for beginners – important to learn from an experienced trainer – important to use the correct swimming gear – lots of clubs where swimming is taught – swimming tournaments draw huge crowds

Conclusion: healthy activity that you can do all your life – helps you to relax and feel good – great way to make friends – young people should be encouraged to take up this activity

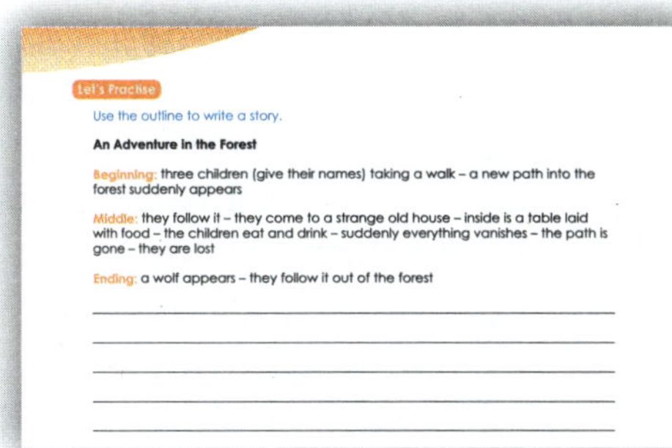

Let's Practise

Use the outline to write a story.

An Adventure in the Forest

Beginning: three children (give their names) taking a walk – a new path into the forest suddenly appears

Middle: they follow it – they come to a strange old house – inside is a table laid with food – the children eat and drink – suddenly everything vanishes – the path is gone – they are lost

Ending: a wolf appears – they follow it out of the forest

Vocabulary building through engaging exercises

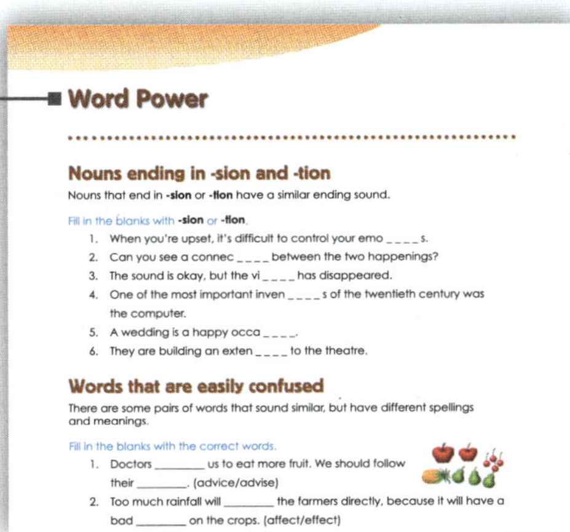

Word Power

Nouns ending in -sion and -tion

Nouns that end in **-sion** or **-tion** have a similar ending sound.

Fill in the blanks with **-sion** or **-tion**.

1. When you're upset, it's difficult to control your emo _ _ _ _ s.
2. Can you see a connec _ _ _ _ between the two happenings?
3. The sound is okay, but the vi _ _ _ _ has disappeared.
4. One of the most important inven _ _ _ _ s of the twentieth century was the computer.
5. A wedding is a happy occa _ _ _ _.
6. They are building an exten _ _ _ _ to the theatre.

Words that are easily confused

There are some pairs of words that sound similar, but have different spellings and meanings.

Fill in the blanks with the correct words.

1. Doctors ________ us to eat more fruit. We should follow their ________. (advice/advise)
2. Too much rainfall will ________ the farmers directly, because it will have a bad ________ on the crops. (affect/effect)

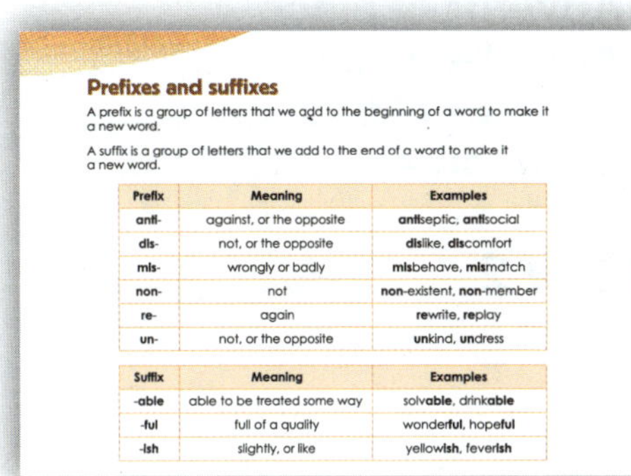

Prefixes and suffixes

A prefix is a group of letters that we add to the beginning of a word to make it a new word.

A suffix is a group of letters that we add to the end of a word to make it a new word.

Prefix	Meaning	Examples
anti-	against, or the opposite	**anti**septic, **anti**social
dis-	not, or the opposite	**dis**like, **dis**comfort
mis-	wrongly or badly	**mis**behave, **mis**match
non-	not	**non**-existent, **non**-member
re-	again	**re**write, **re**play
un-	not, or the opposite	**un**kind, **un**dress

Suffix	Meaning	Examples
-able	able to be treated some way	solv**able**, drink**able**
-ful	full of a quality	wonder**ful**, hope**ful**
-ish	slightly, or like	yellow**ish**, fever**ish**

 ISBN 978-93-5103-602-9

Contents

 ISBN 978-93-5103-602-9

 ISBN 978-93-5103-602-9

1 Nouns

Let's Recall

- **Common nouns** are names for people, places, animals and things.
- **Proper nouns** are names for particular people, places, animals and things.
- Nouns are either **singular** (one) or **plural** (more than one). Some nouns have plurals that are quite different from their singular forms. These are **irregular plurals**.
- **Countable nouns** are things that can be made plural and can be counted.
- **Uncountable nouns** are things that are singular but cannot be counted.
- **Collective nouns** are words for groups of people, animals and things.
- **Masculine nouns** refer to males and **feminine nouns** refer to females.
- Nouns that can be used to refer to both males and females are called **common-gender nouns**.
- We add **'s** after singular nouns and names to show belonging or possession. With plural nouns that end in **-s**, we only add the apostrophe ('). This is called the **possessive** form of the noun.

1.1 Revising nouns

1. Look at the underlined word in each sentence. Then tick the correct box.

	Common noun	Proper noun
a. Dad drove the van to New Delhi.	☐	☐
b. Please send the letter to Mr Biswas.	☐	☐
c. The whale shark is a large fish.	☐	☐
d. Cathy saw a huge castle on the hillside.	☐	☐
e. Let's sit beside the fountains.	☐	☐
f. My cousin lives in Tokyo.	☐	☐

2. Match the **common nouns** with the **proper nouns**.

a. a river •		• i. Chennai
b. a mountain peak •		• ii. Thailand
c. a country •		• iii. the Taj Mahal
d. a city •		• iv. Nelson Mandela
e. a building •		• v. Mt Everest
f. a leader •		• vi. the Nile

 ISBN 978-93-5103-602-9

3. Circle the **singular nouns** and underline the **plural nouns**.

a. We have two guitars, a piano and a violin in our house.

b. Grandmother grows many different plants in her garden.

c. There are several buses that go to Agra.

d. Grandfather collects stamps and watches.

e. Rina loves mangoes and oranges, but she doesn't like bananas.

f. Our cat enjoys playing with his little ball. Sometimes he chews my shoes.

4. Fill in the blanks with the **plural** form of the **noun** given in the brackets.

The Varma family were going for a picnic. Mrs Varma made twelve tomato-and-lettuce ________________ (sandwich). Simran put fruit and cakes in all the ________________ (lunch box). She packed some ________________ (glass) and ________________ (dish) too. Geeta put all the hats and ________________ (scarf) in a large bag. Rohit and Dilip took down their favourite books from the ________________ (shelf) and packed them in their rucksacks. Simran wrapped the forks and ________________ (knife) in thick paper and put them into the picnic basket. Now they were ready to set off!

Remember!
For nouns that end in **-s**, **-ss**, **-o**, **-x**, **-ch** or **-sh**, we add **-es** to make them plural. Some nouns ending in **-f** or **-fe** change **-f** or **-fe** to **-ves**.

5. Circle the incorrect **plural nouns**. Write the correct plural form in each blank.

a. Please stack the cardboard boxs in the corner. ________________

b. We chew our food with our tooths. ________________

c. The gooses on my uncle's farm love cabbage! ________________

d. We enjoy listening to Grandmother's storys. ________________

e. May I have some strawberrys? ________________

f. Cats like chasing mouses. ________________

g. We saw a lot of aircrafts in the sky on Republic Day. ________________

h. There are only five loafs of bread left in the shop. ________________

i. Foxs have bushy tails. ________________

j. Ruby and Benny saw a large number of deers in the park. ________________

Remember!
The spelling of some nouns are changed to form the plural. Some nouns, such as **deer** and **aircraft**, have a plural that is the same as the singular. Some nouns, such as **shorts**, are always plural.

 ISBN 978-93-5103-602-9

6. Look at each underlined noun. In the brackets, write **C** for countable nouns or **UC** for uncountable nouns.

a. I have a lot of <u>homework</u> today. [ ]

b. We played three <u>games</u> of badminton. [ ]

c. Shannon is afraid of any <u>insect</u> that flies. [ ]

d. The nicest dessert is strawberries with <u>cream</u>. [ ]

e. Joe lay down on the <u>grass</u>. [ ]

f. There was a lively <u>band</u> in the restaurant, playing great music. [ ]

g. May I have some <u>jam</u> on my bread, please? [ ]

h. The furniture shop sells a great variety of <u>chairs</u>. [ ]

Take Note
We can use phrases, such as **a piece of**, **a slice of**, **a cup of**, before uncountable nouns.

7. Fill in the blanks with the correct words from the box below.

bread	pineapple	biscuits	juice
soap	milk	flour	cake	coffee

Zara and Zayn went to the supermarket on Sunday. They picked up four bars of _______________, a loaf of _______________, a bag of _______________, two bottles of _______________ and a packet of _______________. Then they bought six cartons of _______________ and a tin of sliced _______________. "There, that completes the list!" said Zara. "Let's go to the billing counter now. After that, let's have a cup of _______________ and a slice of _______________."

8. Match the group of words with the correct **collective noun**.

a. a pile of •	• i. flats
b. a string of •	• ii. ships
c. a block of •	• iii. beads
d. a crowd of •	• iv. newspapers
e. a fleet of •	• v. photographers

Take Note
We can use **flock** or **flight** for several kinds of birds, such as pigeons and geese.

9. Circle the correct **collective noun** to complete each sentence.

a. We watched a (flock / army) of birds flying across the sky.

b. The thief was attacked by a (pack / swarm) of bees.

c. A large (herd / gang) of elephants gathered round the hunters.

d. Henry gave me a (bunch / collection) of roses on my birthday.

e. A colourful (group / school) of fish twisted and turned through the water.

 ISBN 978-93-5103-602-9

10. Fill in each blank with a suitable **collective noun** from the box below. Then circle the correct verb.

staff	team	family	troop	committee

a. The ________________ (march / marches) in time with the music.

b. The ________________ (consist / consists) of two managers and five sales assistants.

c. The housing ________________ (hold / holds) a meeting every month.

d. Our ________________ (has / have) been practising very hard for the tournament.

e. My ________________ (comes / come) together every year from all over the world to celebrate Christmas.

Take Note
A collective noun is singular, but can be used with a plural verb if it sounds more sensible, e.g. The audience **were** clapping loudly. A crowd of children **are** crossing the road.

11. Fill in each blank with a suitable **masculine** or **feminine noun** from the box below.

lioness	bridegroom	gentlemen
waitress	peahens	princesses

a. Princes are expected to marry ________________.

b. A boy bumped into the ________________ and she dropped a pile of plates.

c. The ________________ usually hunts for food while the lion protects the pride.

d. Peacocks are colourful, whereas ________________ are usually dull-coloured.

e. Ladies and ________________, please take your seats.

f. The bride and ________________ received some lovely wedding presents.

12. Rewrite each sentence by replacing the underlined noun with a noun of the opposite **gender**. Make other changes as necessary.

a. The <u>gander</u> has a long neck and a short broad bill.

____

b. The <u>emperor</u> was very fond of his jewels.

____

c. The <u>stewardess</u> said that she would get a new headset for me.

____

d. I heard my <u>landlord</u> having an argument with his <u>wife</u>.

____

e. He was a powerful <u>wizard</u> and was known for his magic spells.

____

 ISBN 978-93-5103-602-9

13. Fill in the blanks with suitable **common-gender nouns** from the box below.

child	receptionist	parents	children	doctor

Last Saturday, my ________________ and I took my sister to the hospital for a vaccination shot. The ________________ asked us to wait in the lounge. There were several other ________________ waiting for their turn. The ________________ was very gentle with the children, and gave each ________________ a chocolate after the vaccination.

14. Underline the **common-gender nouns**.

Mr Aziz had five grandchildren who lived close by. One day, Mr Aziz asked them what they wanted to be when they grew up.
"I would like to become a pilot, like Papa," said Rehaan. "What about you, Laila?"
"I would like to become a scientist, like Mamma," said Laila. "What are your plans, Amir?"
"Oh, I want to be a veterinarian and open a hospital for animals," Amir said with a smile.
Sania said, "I want to be a photographer and travel all over the world."
"And I love cricket! One day I will be the best cricketer in the world," cried little Usman.

Remember!
A common-gender noun always refers to a living being.

15. Rewrite each group of words using the **possessive** form of the **noun**.

Example the skin of a hippopotamus: a hippopotamus's skin

a. a school for girls: ________________
b. the computer belonging to Jess: ________________
c. the wedding of Diana and Charles: ________________
d. the purse belonging to Miss Rao: ________________
e. a doctor who treats children: ________________
f. the names of the winners: ________________
g. the washroom used by ladies: ________________
h. the streets of Paris: ________________
i. a hostel for boys: ________________
j. the weapons of the soldiers: ________________

Remember!
When two nouns are joined using **and**, we add **'s** after the second noun to show that the thing belongs to both of them.

 ISBN 978-93-5103-602-9

16. Fill in the blanks with the **possessive** form of the **nouns** from the box below.

Tanya	neighbour	sisters	boys	mother
children	friend	James	Sharma	

A new family has moved into our neighbourhood. The ______________ names are Rohit, Ankita and Tanya. Ankita and Tanya are twins. Rohit is Ankita and ______________ younger brother. He does not like joining in his ______________ games. He goes to his ______________ house instead. His friend is called James. Rohit likes ______________ family, and loves his ______________ cooking! One day, while playing cricket, James hit the ball for a six. CRASH! The ball smashed through the ______________ window. The neighbour, old Mrs Sharma, came rushing out with a stick. James and Rohit apologised at once. The ______________ parents promised to repair Mrs ______________ window.

17. Circle the correct **possessive** form of the **noun** to complete each sentence.

a. She borrowed her (mothers' / mother's) bag for the party.

b. A sign on the (librarian's / librarians') desk warned that students would have to pay a fine if books were returned late.

c. The porter loaded the four (gentlemen's / gentlemens') bags onto the trolley.

d. The (waitresses' / waitress's) apron was stained, so she put on a clean one.

e. For the celebrations on Annual Day, all (parent's / parents') cars must be parked in the parking lot behind the auditorium.

f. The (girl's / girls') mobile phone kept ringing, but she refused to take the call.

Take Note
With irregular plurals that don't end in **-s**, we add **'s** as for singular nouns.

18. Use each word pair to make a sentence. Use the first noun in its **possessive** form.

a. teacher room

____

b. scouts tents

____

c. princess crown

____

 ISBN 978-93-5103-602-9

1.2 Neuter nouns

Read the story.

A boy and a girl went to visit a **castle** with their parents. It was a lovely sunny **day**.

The **rooms** in the **castle** were decorated with beautiful **paintings**.

After the **tour**, the guide led them into a sunny **garden** with a **fountain** and **flowers**.

Remember!
Nouns that refer to males are called **masculine nouns** and those that refer to females are called **feminine nouns**. Nouns that can mean a male or a female are called **common-gender nouns**, e.g. parent, child, teacher.

What else do you think the children saw in the garden?

What were the family visiting?

What did they see in the tour?

Where did they go after the tour? What did they see there?

1. From the story above, find an example of the following.
   a. A noun that refers to a male: ____________
   b. A noun that refers to a female: ____________
   c. A noun that can refer to both a male and a female: ____________
   d. A noun that refers to a thing: ____________

2. Underline the nouns that refer to things in the sentence.
   a. Sally sat under a tree reading a book.
   b. The taps in the kitchen need to be repaired.
   c. They packed their bags and took a taxi to the station.
   d. We bought a new computer last week.
   e. She found an old map in the basement.

Nouns that are names for non-living things are called **neuter nouns**. The word neuter means neither male nor female.

 ISBN 978-93-5103-602-9

Let's Practise

A. Circle the **common-gender nouns** and underline the **neuter nouns**.

doctor	dancer	picture	Dubai	lawyer
student	person	magazine	writer	pile
teacher	Kolkata	friend	diaries	umbrella
computer	child	boot	doll	cook
driver	wheels	bunch	pilot	hairdresser

Take Note

- A neuter noun can be singular, plural or collective.
- Names for places are also neuter nouns.

B. Read the story. Then list the **common-gender nouns** and the **neuter nouns** in the table below.

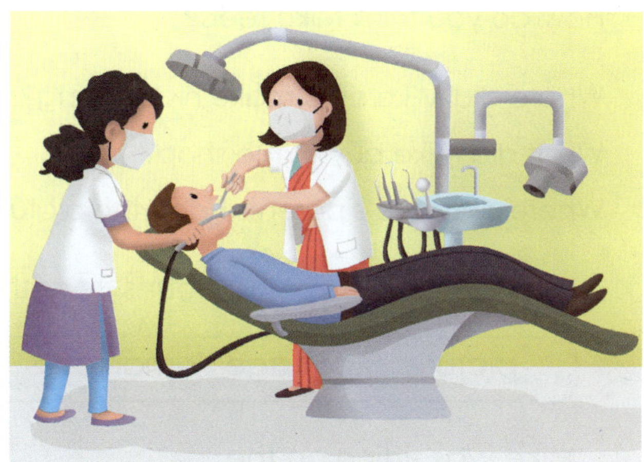

Mr Sinha had a sore tooth, so he went to his dentist, Dr Mehta. The receptionist showed him into the examination room. Dr Mehta asked him to sit in the chair and open his mouth wide. "There's a cavity that must be filled," she said. She told her assistant to spray his mouth with water and began drilling the tooth.

"Mmm...mmm," mumbled Mr Sinha.

"Relax, it will soon be over," said the dentist. "There, it's done now!"

"But that's the wrong tooth!" cried Mr Sinha. "The sore tooth was on the left!"

Common-gender nouns	Neuter nouns

 ISBN 978-93-5103-602-9

1.3 Concrete nouns

Remember!
Countable nouns are things that can be counted and can be made plural. Uncountable nouns are things that cannot be counted.

Read the story.

Mike was sitting in the **garden** making a **painting** of his **house** to give to his mum and dad.

He went to a **shop** with his parents to choose a **frame** for his **picture**.

They hung the **picture** behind the **sofa** in the **living room**.

How do you think Mike feels?

Where did Mike sit to make his painting?

What did Mike buy at the shop?

Where did Mike's parents hang the picture?

1. Rewrite the story using nouns from the box below.

picture cottage market couch sitting room sketch lawn

Mike was sitting on the ______________ making a ______________ of his ______________ to give to his mum and dad. He went to the ______________ with his parents to choose a frame for his ______________. They hung the picture behind the ______________ in their ______________.

2. Circle the nouns that you can see or touch.

cloud	dictionary	ice	telephone	scissors
rule	joke	paper	trick	mug
holiday	carpet	prayer	needle	hair
finger	minute	honour	example	roof

Nouns for things that we can see or touch are called **concrete nouns**. Concrete nouns can be countable or uncountable.

 ISBN 978-93-5103-602-9

Let's Practise

A. Circle all the **concrete nouns** in the story and list them under the correct headings below.

Mum handed Dinesh a list of goods she wanted from the shops. He rode his bicycle down to the chemist and bought a strip of tablets for Grandfather, three bars of soap, a sponge and a roll of toilet paper. Then he rode to the grocery and bought a bag of flour, four oranges, some potatoes, some rice and some milk. Finally he rode back to his house and put all the shopping bags on the table.

Concrete countable nouns		Concrete uncountable nouns	

B. Unscramble the letters in the brackets to find the correct **concrete noun**. Write it in the blank.

1. We're having banana pie for (tssdere) this evening. __________
2. The old lady in the red cardigan lost her (epsur) while shopping at the supermarket. __________
3. Sheila, the girl with the (tponlaiy), was top of the class in Maths last year. __________
4. The house needs a new coat of (npiat). __________
5. Mr Das helped the police to arrest the (fhtie). __________

 ISBN 978-93-5103-602-9

1.4 Abstract nouns

Remember!
Names of people, places, animals and things are all nouns. Concrete nouns are things that we can see or touch.

Read the story.

Roy and his friends were having **fun** playing a **game** on the beach.

They got a **fright** when the water surrounded them. They were in **danger** and they yelled for **help**.

By good **luck**, two men in a motor boat heard them, rescued them and brought them to **safety**.

What do you think happened next?

What were the children doing on the beach?

What happened when the water surrounded them?

How did the men help them?

1. Read the story again and list all the nouns in the blanks below. Then circle the nouns that you cannot see or touch.

________	________	________	________
________	________	________	________
________	________	________	________
________	________	________	________

2. Circle the nouns that are NOT concrete.

reason	mat	ceiling	day	idea	mistake
table	collar	rule	voice	love	star
pan	clock	vacation	song	beak	aim
toy	map	insect	fire	jug	memory

Nouns for things that we can't see or touch are called **abstract nouns**.

 ISBN 978-93-5103-602-9

Abstract nouns can be formed from verbs, adjectives and other nouns. Here are some of the common endings that these abstract nouns have.

-ness

Adjective	Noun	Adjective	Noun
bold	boldness	happy	happiness
dark	darkness	lazy	laziness
friendly	friendliness	shy	shyness
great	greatness	ugly	ugliness

Take Note
For adjectives that end in **-y**, we change the **-y** to **-i** and add **-ness**, e.g. **silly**, **silliness**. However, for the adjectives **dry**, **shy** and **sly**, we just add **-ness**, e.g. **dryness**, **shyness**, **slyness**.

-ion

Verb	Noun	Verb	Noun
act	action	explore	exploration
create	creation	instruct	instruction
decide	decision	invade	invasion
discuss	discussion	permit	permission
educate	education	solve	solution

-y, -ty, -ity

Adjective	Noun	Adjective	Noun
able	ability	popular	popularity
honest	honesty	real	reality
loyal	loyalty	severe	severity

-ance, -ence

Adjective	Noun	Verb	Noun
brilliant	brilliance	appear	appearance
different	difference	guide	guidance
elegant	elegance	refer	reference

-hood

Noun	Noun	Adjective	Noun
adult	adulthood	false	falsehood
child	childhood	likely	likelihood

Think & Share Get into groups of ten. Make a list of concrete uncountable nouns, for example, sugar, milk, and abstract countable nouns, for example, question, joke. Compare your lists and highlight all the nouns that are common to all the groups. Then each group tells a story to the class using the highlighted nouns.

 ISBN 978-93-5103-602-9

Let's Practise

A. Underline the **abstract noun(s)** in each sentence.

1. Janet was well known in school for her smartness and intelligence.
2. This book is about the mysteries of outer space.
3. The clown was so funny that the audience roared with laughter.
4. We must take pride in what we do.
5. Sir Hector was known the world over for his great strength and bravery.

B. Fill in each blank with an **abstract noun** formed from the word given in the brackets.

1. Jane's heart swelled with __________ (happy).
2. When making your own greeting cards, be sure to select paper of the right __________ (thick).
3. This project cannot be completed without the full __________ (cooperate) of all the team members.
4. Heidi had a happy __________ (child) in the beautiful Alpine mountains.
5. The mysterious __________ (disappear) of Nina's puppy is worrying.

C. Circle the **nouns** in the story. Then list them under the correct headings below.

At our school we have classes in Maths, Art, Music, History and other subjects. Today in English we learnt about words called nouns. They are names for people, places, animals and things, and also for qualities, such as truth, beauty and skill. Our teacher wrote them in chalk on the blackboard.

Take Note
Abstract nouns include the names of school subjects.

Concrete	**Concrete**	**Abstract**	**Abstract**
________	________	________	________
________	________	________	________
________	________	________	________
________	________	________	________
________	________	________	________
________	________	________	________
________	________	________	________

ISBN 978-93-5103-602-9

1.5 Compound nouns

Read the story.

Jenny and Louise were in a **coffee bar**. Jenny couldn't drink her lemonade as she had **toothache**.

The next day Jenny went to the dentist for a **check-up**. He said the pain was a result of **tooth decay**.

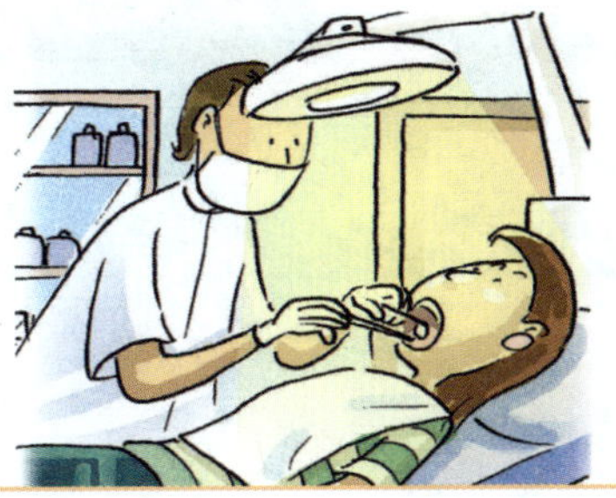

He used a **toothbrush** and a set of **false teeth** to show Jenny how to clean her teeth properly.

What is a good title for the story?

Where were Jenny and Louise?

Why did Jenny go to the dentist?

What two things did the dentist use?

1. Note the highlighted nouns in the story above. Now underline each noun that consists of two words.

   a. Too much sugar causes tooth decay.

   b. Jenny had to go for a dental check-up.

   c. Jenny sat for a while in the waiting room.

   d. The dentist was wearing a face mask.

2. Combine the two highlighted words in each sentence below and write the noun formed.

   Example A **frame** for a **picture** is a picture frame.

   a. A **case** for **pencils** is a ____________.

   b. A **suit** for **diving** is a ____________.

   c. **Shoes** for **gym** are ____________.

   d. **Shoes** for **running** are ____________.

A noun that is made up of two words is a **compound noun**. Compound nouns may be written as one word, with a space between the words or with a dash (-) between the words.

 ISBN 978-93-5103-602-9

Compound nouns can be formed with a verb, an adjective or another noun. Here are some compound nouns formed in these ways.

with verb (-ing)
dining room
diving board
driving licence
frying pan
magnifying glass
parking light
shaving cream
sleeping bag
swimming pool
washing machine

Take Note
In order to form the plural of a compound noun with a space between words, we use the correct plural form of the second word, e.g. **tennis shoes**. In order to form the plural of a compound noun like passer-by, we add **-s** to the first word, e.g. **passer-by** becomes **passers-by**, **runner-up** becomes **runners-up**.

with adjective
blue whale
common sense
false teeth
full moon
high five
mobile phone
right angle
superstar
yellow fever

with noun
bath mat
book club
face cream
fire engine
fish tank
football
ocean basin
paper weight
railway bridge
smoke alarm
sunflower
table lamp
window frame

 ISBN 978-93-5103-602-9

Let's Practise

A. Match the words to make **compound nouns**.

1. play	•	•	a. port
2. lawn	•	•	b. washer
3. dish	•	•	c. board
4. key	•	•	d. ground
5. air	•	•	e. mower

B. Combine the highlighted words and fill in each blank with the correct **compound noun**.

1. A **box** for **toys** is a ______________________.
2. A **basket** for **bread** is a ______________________.
3. A **bin** for **rubbish** is a ______________________.
4. A **centre** for **shopping** is a ______________________.
5. A **bear** that is **black** is a ______________________.

C. Make a **compound noun** from the highlighted words below.

Example A person that **drives** a **taxi** is a taxi-driver.

1. A tool for **straightening hair** is a ______________________.
2. A tool for **opening tins** is a ______________________.
3. A padded jacket that **warms** your **body** is a ______________________.
4. A person who **attends** to passengers on a **flight** is a ______________________.

D. Make a sentence with each **compound noun**.

1. dancing shoes

____

____

2. fishing rod

____

____

3. blue whale

____

____

 ISBN 978-93-5103-602-9

2 Pronouns

Let's Recall

- **Pronouns** are words that take the place of nouns in a sentence.
- **I, we, you, he, she, it, they, me, us, him, her** and **them** are called **personal pronouns**.
- **I, me, we** and **us** refer to the people speaking. They are called **first-person pronouns**.
- **You** refers to the person or people spoken to. This is the **second-person pronoun**.
- The words **this, that, these** and **those** are also used in place of nouns. They are called **demonstrative pronouns**. We use **this** (singular) and **these** (plural) to talk about things near us. We use **that** (singular) and **those** (plural) to talk about things that are at a distance.

2.1 Revising pronouns

1. Fill in each blank with the correct **personal pronoun**.

   a. Mary has a sore tooth. Dad is taking _____ to the dentist.

   b. Please answer the phone if _____ rings.

   c. Hurry up, children! Your parents are waiting for _____.

   d. Mr Jones is a good teacher. _____ teaches grammar.

   e. Mala and I are sisters. _____ go to the same school.

   f. May _____ move my desk, please?

   g. What are _____ looking for, Kate?

   h. All Miss Mirren's students like _____.

   i. This is my cousin Sujit. _____ plays the guitar.

   j. The Bhatias have just bought a house. _____ is by the beach.

Remember!
You is both a singular and a plural pronoun. We can say
- You must pay attention, Anna!
- You must pay attention, children!

2. Fill in the blanks with **pronouns** that can be used in place of the nouns given in the brackets.

   Joe called Jack and asked _____ (Jack), "Would you like to see a film with _____ (Joe) tomorrow?"

   Jack said _____ (Jack) had flu and couldn't come. Then Joe called Katy, who said _____ (Katy) could come with _____ (Joe), if her mum would let _____ (Katy). Next, Joe called his other friends Sally and Ken, and asked _____ (Sally and Ken) if _____ (Sally and Ken) wanted to come too.

 ISBN 978-93-5103-602-9

"Oh yes, _____ (Sally and Ken) would love to come!" _____ (Sally and Ken) said.

"Please book two seats for _____ (Sally and Ken)!"

Sally and Ken asked Joe what time the film started.

"_____ (The film) starts at 6.30," said Joe, "so _____ (Joe) shall see _____ (Sally and Ken) then."

3. Circle the correct **demonstrative pronoun** to complete each sentence.

a. "(Those / These) are geese," said Tina, pointing to the birds flying in the sky.

b. These bags are cheap, but (these / those) over there are very expensive.

c. This shop has a large variety of shoes. (Those / that) are for regular wear and (this / these) are for party wear.

d. You've mixed up our swimsuits again! (This / These) is mine and (these / that) is yours.

e. Who is (those / that) knocking at the door?

4. Fill in the blanks with **this**, **that**, **these** or **those**.

Rachel wanted some modern-history books for her school project, so she went to the neighbourhood library. She stretched up to reach a book on the top shelf.

"Oh! __________ is too high. I can't reach it," she said.

"May I help?" said the librarian. She brought it down for her and asked, "Is __________ the book you wanted?"

"Yes, it is. Thank you," Rachel replied, smiling. "Are __________ all the history books you have?"

"__________ are the books on ancient history," she replied, pointing at the shelves in front of her.

"__________ over there are the ones on modern history," she added.

"Then, __________ is where I should be looking," said Rachel, walking towards those shelves.

 ISBN 978-93-5103-602-9

2.2 Third-person pronouns

Read the story.

Peter was camping out with Harry. **He** asked Harry to help **him** put up the tent.

"**It** will be wet and windy tonight," said the weatherman.

Mum saw the boys creeping into the house. **She** woke Dad. **They** decided to say nothing.

Remember!

I, **me**, **we** and **us** refer to the people speaking. They are called **first-person pronouns**. **You** refers to the person or people spoken to. This is the **second-person pronoun**.

Do you think Peter and Harry will camp out again? Why do you think so?

How did Harry help Peter?

What did the weatherman say about the weather?

What did Mum do when she saw the boys creeping into the house?

1. Fill in the blanks with pronouns from the story above.

Peter and Harry decided to camp in the back garden. Peter brought out the tent ______ had got on his birthday last year. The boys were busy putting up the tent, so ______ did not hear the weather forecast on the television. ______ said there would be a terrible storm that night. Around midnight, Mum heard a sound. ______ woke Dad and ______ peered out to see the boys going to their room, dripping wet!

2. Fill in each blank with a pronoun.

a. Sara and Ira are sisters. ______ share a bedroom.
b. Please feed the cat if ______ seems hungry.
c. Mr Khan is a teacher. ______ teaches English.
d. Meet Harry and Peter. ______ are our next-door neighbours.
e. Mum is a doctor. ______ works in a hospital.

He, **she**, **it**, **they**, **him**, **her** and **them** are pronouns that refer to the people or things that we are speaking about. They are called **third-person pronouns**.

 ISBN 978-93-5103-602-9

Let's Practise

A. Fill in the blanks with **third-person pronouns**.

Sally went round to see Billy, but _____ got no answer when _____ rang the bell. _____ was turning away to go back home when suddenly _____ appeared from behind the house. _____ had been working in the garden and hadn't heard _____ ringing the bell. "Come into the kitchen for some coffee," _____ said. Billy made _____ both coffee. _____ chatted for about an hour. Then Sally stood up, saying _____ was time for _____ to go, and _____ dashed off.

B. Circle the correct **pronoun** to complete each sentence.

1. Priya has a slight fever, so Mum is taking (she / her) to see a doctor.
2. All Mr Cooper's neighbours like (him / he).
3. I picked up the books and put (him / them) away.
4. Take an umbrella in case (it / them) rains.
5. Kapil is upset because (he / him) lost the race.
6. Rita thought (she / her) knew the right answer.

C. Rewrite each sentence. Replace the underlined words with **it**.

Example The time is five thirty.

It is five thirty.

1. The weather is warm and sunny today.

____

2. Where's my mobile? Your mobile is on the table.

____

3. Don't talk loudly. Talking loudly disturbs others.

____

4. The time is already seven o'clock.

____

Take Note

The pronoun **it** is used for many purposes, e.g. to talk about the weather, to tell the time or to talk about a situation.

 ISBN 978-93-5103-602-9

2.3 Possessive pronouns

Read the story.

Mum found empty drink cans in the dustbin. "Those were **mine**!" cried Kiran.

"Did you take Kiran's drink cans, Rohan?" asked Mum. "Yes, I didn't know they were **hers**," said Rohan.

"You shouldn't take something that is not **yours**," said Mum.

What do you think Rohan should do next?

What did Kiran say when she saw the empty drink cans?

Why did Rohan take the cans? What did he tell Mum?

What did Mum tell Rohan?

1. Note the highlighted pronouns in the story above. Now circle the pronouns that show possession.

   a. Rohan took some drink cans that were not his.

   b. Kiran told Mum the drink cans were hers.

   c. The friends didn't know the cans weren't theirs to drink.

   d. Are these drink cans ours or yours?

2. Fill in each blank with a pronoun from the box below.

hers	mine	yours	ours	theirs	his

   a. The books on the desk are ________. They belong to me.

   b. This cup belongs to Geeta. It is ________.

   c. The green bag over there is ________. He bought it this morning.

   d. The sweaters on that bed are theirs. The jackets on this bed are ________.

   e. The cakes are ________. They baked them yesterday.

   f. I have lost my pencil. Can I borrow ________?

A pronoun that shows possession is called a **possessive pronoun**.

 ISBN 978-93-5103-602-9

Let's Practise

A. Fill in each blank with a **possessive pronoun** from the box below.

his	mine	yours	hers	theirs	ours	yours	hers

Take Note
Possessive pronouns stand on their own. They are not used before a noun. We do not use an apostrophe with possessive pronouns.

1. This is not the Smiths' car. It is _______.
2. I've already had my lunch, but Sally will have _______ a little later.
3. This is not my book. Is it _______?
4. We gave our new neighbours our telephone numbers, and they gave us _______.
5. This desk is _______. Please don't put your things on it.
6. Did you two order these pizzas? Are they _______?
7. This bicycle belongs to Harry. It is _______.
8. These jeans can't be Jenny's. _______ are in the washing machine.

B. Complete each sentence with **of** and a **possessive pronoun** from the box below.

theirs	his	hers	mine	yours	ours

1. My mum makes very good plum pudding. It's a favourite recipe _______________.
2. Yes, I know Anjali very well. She's a good friend _______________.
3. Thank you, Ajay. That idea _______________ is worth considering.
4. Vikas went into town to meet a few friends _______________.
5. Rachel is related to John and me. I think she's a cousin _______________.
6. Mr Arora and Mrs Shetty are taking some students _______________ to the theatre.

Think & Share Get into groups of five and play the "Bag Game". Sit in a circle and put your school bags in the centre. Lightly blindfold a student and ask them to pick up a bag, take it to each student in the circle and ask, "Is this bag **yours**?" If it is not the student's bag, they reply, "No, it's not **mine**. It may be **hers/his**." Finally, the student who owns the bag says, "Yes, this bag is **mine**."

 ISBN 978-93-5103-602-9

3 Articles

Let's Recall

- The words **a**, **an** and **the** are **articles**. They are used before nouns. **An** is used when the noun begins with a vowel or vowel sound.
- **A** and **an** are used when they do not refer to any particular noun. They are called **indefinite articles. The** is used to refer to a particular noun. It is called a **definite article**. It is used before singular and plural nouns.

3.1 Revising articles

1. Circle the correct **articles** to complete the story.

Last Sunday was (a / an) day to remember! We visited (the / a) National Aquarium in our city. We took (the / an) elevator to (the / a) first floor. We saw (a / an) octopus and lots of other strange sea creatures. I really enjoyed feeding fish to (a / an) dolphin. The last thing we saw was (an / a) exhibition about (the / an) ocean floor.

2. Fill in the blanks with **articles**.

Phil went into ____ sitting room and sat down on ____ sofa. He used ____ remote control to turn on ____ television. There was ____ loud noise in ____ corridor outside. It was his mother using ____ vacuum cleaner. He got up and closed ____ door. Then he settled down to watch ____ programme about ____ animal called ____ kinkajou. Suddenly, ____ telephone rang. It was his father calling up to say he would be ____ hour late. A few minutes later, ____ doorbell rang. Phil switched off ____ television in disgust. "I can't even watch ____ programme in peace!" he sighed.

Remember!

We use **the** before a noun when we are talking about something or someone definite. In such cases, our hearers know which thing or person we mean, usually because there is only one that we could possibly mean, e.g. Please close **the** door.

 ISBN 978-93-5103-602-9

3.2 More about articles

Read the story.

Alice and Joe were on **holiday**. The road to the railway station was jammed with **vehicles**.

Alice and Joe waited on the platform. They were going to travel by **train** to the mountains.

The train was crowded with **tourists**. "We should have gone by **air**," sighed Alice.

How do you think Alice and Joe feel at the start of their holiday?

Why were Alice and Joe going to the mountains?

How were they going to travel to the mountains?

What did Alice say when she saw the crowd inside the train?

1. Note the highlighted words in the story above. Now circle the suitable words to complete each sentence.

   a. Alice and Joe were on (a holiday / holiday).

   b. Alice and Joe prefer travelling by train to travelling by (car / the car).

   c. Too many cars cause (traffic jams / the traffic jams).

   d. The train they boarded was full of (tourists / the tourists).

   e. Alice thought it would have been better to go by (air / the air).

Remember!
Famous objects are sometimes used with **the**, e.g. **the** Taj Mahal, **the** *Mona Lisa*.

2. Rearrange each group of words to make a complete sentence.

   a. I go to don't want to school today

   ____

   b. goes Nita work to bus by

   ____

   c. games children playing computer enjoy

   ____

   d. for three weeks Joe in hospital had to stay

   ____

   e. Australia commonly are kangaroos found in

   ____

Plural nouns and uncountable nouns can be used **without an article**. The names of most places are used without an article.

ISBN 978-93-5103-602-9

Let's Practise

A. Circle the correct words to complete each sentence.

1. The Earth is mostly covered with (water / the water).
2. We went to (London / the London) and visited (British Museum / the British Museum).
3. I prefer the blue dress because (blue / the blue) is my favourite colour.
4. Would you like (tea / the tea) or coffee?
5. I'd like to visit (America / the America) and see (the Statue of Liberty / Statue of Liberty).

B. Complete the story with suitable nouns from the box below. Add an **article** where needed.

tube	bathroom	bedroom	ghosts
water	shower	cupboard	bed
party	Halloween	sheet	clothes

It was the morning of ___________. Laura got out of ___________ and stretched. Then she went to ___________ to wash. She couldn't find ___________ of toothpaste, so she brushed her teeth with soap! She turned on ___________, but she found that ___________ was cold. Shivering, she went back to ___________ and opened ___________. Oh dear! It was filled with dirty ___________! What would she wear for ___________ tonight? Then she thought, "___________ are white. I'll just take ___________ off the bed and wear it and pretend I'm a ghost!"

Take Note
Some countable nouns are used without an article, especially after certain prepositions. They include various means of transport, such as bus and car, and places, such as school and bed. However, they need an article when we mean a particular means of transport or place, e.g. Dad goes everywhere **by car**. He parks **the car** outside in the street.

C. Cross out the **articles** where they are not needed.

1. I study the History and the Geography at the school.
2. Did you come by car or by the bike?
3. I enjoy learning the languages. I can speak the English and the Tamil.
4. Let's meet at the breakfast and then decide the plan for the day.
5. Owls and bats are most active at the night.

 ISBN 978-93-5103-602-9

Review 1

1. Circle the **neuter nouns** in the table. Make sentences with any five.

book	child	driver	shoes	stone	doctor
sun	pen	computer	teacher	baby	enemy
mother	mouse	paper	lion	uncle	tree
cow	author	friend	pilot	star	apple

a. ____

____

b. ____

____

c. ____

____

d. ____

____

e. ____

____

2. Look at each underlined word. In the brackets, write **C** if it is a concrete noun or **A** if it is an abstract noun.

a. Ria looked at her work and smiled in satisfaction. [ ]

b. Dad took a photo of me riding a camel. [ ]

c. Learning to play the guitar requires patience. [ ]

d. Her eyes were full of hope as she waited for the judges to declare the winner. [ ]

e. The lake was covered with ice. [ ]

f. The taxi-driver returned the bag to its owner and was rewarded for his honesty. [ ]

g. There wasn't a speck of dust to be seen anywhere in the house. [ ]

h. I have no idea what the children are doing right now. [ ]

 ISBN 978-93-5103-602-9

3. Fill in the blanks with **abstract nouns** from the box below.

honesty	reaction	surprise	uncertainty	silence
	rudeness	truth	assistance	

Mum was trying on her new dress. She needed my __________ to fasten the zip. Her face expressed __________ as she looked at herself in the mirror. Then she turned round and asked Harry and me, "What do you think of this dress? Tell me the __________, Harry."

Harry looked at Mum in __________. Then he said, "Oh, it looks awful!"

I gasped in __________ at his __________. But Mum's __________ surprised me even more. She was not angry at all. In fact, she praised Harry for his __________.

4. Match the nouns in the two columns to form a **compound noun**.

a. motor •	• i. works
b. text •	• ii. room
c. class •	• iii. cycle
d. fire •	• iv. book

5. Fill in each blank with the correct **compound noun** from the box below.

polar bears	headache	passer-by
	bathroom	

a. A __________ helped the old lady cross the road.

b. A tap is leaking in the __________.

c. __________ live near the North Pole.

d. Grandmother has a __________, so she wants to lie down for a while.

6. Make a sentence with each **compound noun**.

a. storeroom

____

b. school bus

____

c. blackboard

____

  ISBN 978-93-5103-602-9

7. Fill in each blank with a **third-person pronoun**.

a. Sid finally found the potato-peeler, but ______ was broken.

b. Ask Alisha and Divya if ______ would like to go to the wedding with us.

c. Tom refused to have the soup. ______ wanted noodles instead.

d. It was Trisha's birthday, so Mum baked cookies for ______.

e. I've downloaded the film, but just can't find the time to watch ______.

f. It's my parents' anniversary tomorrow. What should I buy for ______?

g. Grandfather is sleeping now. Please don't disturb ______.

h. Pia will be sick if ______ eats any more cakes.

8. Fill in each blank with the correct **possessive pronoun**. The underlined word will help you.

a. Tell me your name, and I will tell you ______.

b. I've finished my work. Have you finished ______?

c. Rima and Rina have made their beds. Has Rohit made ______?

d. You have found your bag, but I haven't found ______.

e. If you both bring your bicycles, we will bring ______.

f. We'll show you our photos after you show us ______.

g. Jane has spent her pocket money, but George hasn't spent ______.

h. The principal smiled at the girl and said he would be glad to meet any friend of ______.

9. Circle the **possessive pronouns** in the story below.

"Are these lunch boxes ours?" asked Sachin.

"No, those are for your dad and me. Yours are on the dining table," replied Mum.

"This one can't be mine," said Diya. "It has a banana in it. I hate bananas."

"So do I," said Sachin. "Dad likes bananas. This box must be his."

Sachin went back to the kitchen and said, "Mum, you gave Dad's lunch box to Diya by mistake, so I'm swapping it for hers."

"Fine," said Mum.

 ISBN 978-93-5103-602-9

10. Circle the correct word to complete each sentence.

a. i. Sam plans to go to (university / the university) next summer.
   ii. I live quite close to (university / the university).

b. i. Are you going to (the church / church) this Sunday?
   ii. (The church / Church) at the end of the road has a beautiful garden.

c. i. The judge sentenced the criminal to three years in (the prison / prison).
   ii. The journalists crowded outside (the prison / prison) in Newtown to get news about the daring escape of twelve convicts.

11. Fill in the blanks with **articles**. Put a zero (**0**) in the blank if an article is not required.

"What would you like for ______ breakfast, children?" asked Dad.

"I'd like ______ jam sandwich and ______ milk," said John.

"I'd like ______ toast and ______ cheese and ______ cup of hot chocolate," Nora said.

"May I have ______ omelette and ______ French fries?" asked Joy.

Dad smiled and said, "No French fries for you, Joy. Why don't you have ______ cereal with ______ fruit and nuts? They give you lots of ______ energy and are tasty too."

Spot the Error

12. There is a mistake in each sentence. Underline it and rewrite the sentence correctly in the blank below.

a. The dentist taught Pooja how to use a tooth brush.

____

b. Jai has finished breakfast, but his sister will have theirs a little later.

____

c. I'll be at the home all evening.

____

d. I can see Mrs Dey's car but where is our's?

____

e. Everyone was puzzled about the sudden disappearence of the cat.

____

f. They plan to travel by the train to Nainital.

____

 ISBN 978-93-5103-602-9

4 Adjectives

Let's Recall

- **Adjectives** describe nouns. Some adjectives describe the material, appearance, age, speed, temperature or quality of nouns.
- We use **this**, **that**, **these** and **those** to point out particular people or things. These words are called **demonstrative adjectives**. They always come before nouns.
- We use **my**, **our**, **your**, **his**, **her**, **its** and **their** to show or ask who or what possesses or has something. They are called **possessive adjectives**. They also come before nouns.
- We use **some**, **a little**, **many** and **much** to express amount and quantity. We also use **numbers** to give the exact amount, for example, **five** kittens. These are all **adjectives of quantity**.
- Adjectives have three forms. When we want to describe someone or something without comparing them with anyone or anything, we use the **positive** form. This is the base form of the adjective. When we compare two nouns, we add **-r** or **-er** to the adjective. This is known as the **comparative** form. When we compare more than two nouns, we add **-est** to the adjective. This is known as the **superlative** form.
- Longer adjectives use **more than** or **the most** to form the comparative and superlative.

4.1 Revising adjectives

1. Fill in each blank with a suitable **adjective** from the box below.

hairy	broken	excited	tiny	dusty

a. Three _______ kittens were curled up on Anya's doorstep.

b. A _______ spider landed beside the little girl and frightened her.

c. An _______ crowd waited outside the auditorium to see the film star.

d. We helped Dad fix the _______ mirror.

e. The toys Sofia found in the loft were _______ and damaged.

2. Think of a person or thing that each **adjective** below can describe. Then use the word pair to make a sentence.

Example healthy food

Nowadays, most department stores stock lots of healthy food.

a. torn ___________

____

 ISBN 978-93-5103-602-9

b. fast __________

____

c. plastic __________

____

d. ancient __________

____

e. icy __________

____

3. Circle the correct **demonstrative adjective** to complete each sentence.

a. I like (that / this) restaurant because the food is really good here.

b. (These / those) red apples here look delicious, but the ones on (these / those) shelves are larger.

c. Can you put (this / these) table over there, please?

d. Please tie up (that / those) garbage bags in the corner.

e. Did you hear (this / that) noise? I think it came from next door.

Take Note
Demonstrative adjectives are used before nouns. **Demonstrative pronouns** are used on their own.

4. Fill in the blanks with **this**, **that**, **these** or **those**.

"Hi, Maya, _____ party is a great idea! Can we help you in any way?"

"Thanks, Vivian, that would be nice. Please take _____ plates and glasses to the table. Rishi, _____ jug over there has some chilled orange juice. Would you please take it round?"

"_____ cutlets are delicious, Maya, and _____ sauce goes so well with them."

"Who took _____ photographs of the Himalayas?"

"Oh, _____ one here was taken by my brother. And I took _____ photograph of the sunset on the wall opposite. Nina, _____ snacks are grilled and _____ snacks on the table are fried. Enjoy yourselves, everyone!"

5. Circle the incorrect **demonstrative adjectives**. Then rewrite the sentences using the correct ones.

a. Look at these tiny insect on my hand!

____

b. The earthquake took place on New Year's Eve. This night, there was a huge storm.

____

 ISBN 978-93-5103-602-9

c. This books over there are the old ones. That books here are new.

____

d. These curry tastes funny. I think you have put too much salt in it.

____

6. Fill in each blank with the correct **possessive adjective** from the box below.

my	her	their	its	our

a. __________ grandparents write to me every month.

b. Susan's dog loves chasing __________ tail.

c. Neha dropped __________ cup and spilt milk on the floor, and the cat promptly lapped it all up!

d. The children do __________ homework as soon as they get home.

e. During __________ next visit to Kashmir, we plan to stay on a houseboat.

Remember!

- The possessive adjectives are **my, your, his, her, its, our,** and **their**.
- The possessive pronouns are **mine, yours, his, hers, ours** and **theirs**. They stand alone and are NOT used before a noun.

7. Circle the **possessive adjectives** in the story.

Chetan rode his bicycle to school and then wheeled it into the bicycle shed. There were already lots of bicycles in the shed. Chetan parked his bicycle at the end of the row. After school, he went to fetch his bicycle. Other children were collecting their bicycles too, but where was his? Just then, Feroz appeared, wheeling a red bicycle. "I've just realised that I took your bicycle by mistake, Chetan," he said. "I'm really sorry."

8. Replace each personal pronoun given in the brackets with the correct **possessive adjective**. Rewrite each sentence.

a. Usha is very fond of (she) dog.

____

b. (He) laptop is quite expensive.

____

c. Could you lend me (you) pen, please?

____

d. (I) favourite hobby is painting.

____

ISBN 978-93-5103-602-9

e. Every year, hundreds of tourists come to Rome to see (it) historical monuments.

____

f. (They) father works in a car factory.

____

9. Fill in each blank with **a little**, **some**, **many** or **much** or a suitable **number**.

Remember! **Many** and **much** are often used with negatives and in questions.

a. There were too ______ children in the pool today.
b. Would you like ______ cold milk with your cereal?
c. Javed is feeling tired because he didn't get ______ sleep last night.
d. There are ______ years in a decade.
e. How ______ glasses do we need for our guests tonight?
f. There was ______ rain this morning, but fortunately the sky soon cleared.

10. Underline the adjectives that show an **amount** or **number** of something in the story below.

Sadia was hungry and wanted to make a quick snack for herself. There were three apples, two oranges and one banana in the fruit basket. She decided to make a fruit salad. She chopped the fruit and added some nuts. There was a little fresh cream in a bowl. She stirred some sugar into it and poured it over the fruit. Then she sat down to eat. She tasted the fruit salad and choked. She had put salt in the cream instead of sugar!

11. Make a sentence with each **adjective of quantity**.

a. a little

____

b. much

____

c. many

____

d. only two

____

e. ten

____

 ISBN 978-93-5103-602-9

4.2 More about adjectives of quantity

Read the story.

There were **several** racks of postcards in the shop. Susie bought postcards to send to **all** her friends.

She wrote **a few** lines describing her holiday. Now she had to buy **a few** stamps.

Susie looked into her purse, but there wasn't **any** money in it! She had been robbed!

What do you think Susie did next?

How many racks of postcards were in the shop?

What did Susie write on the postcards?

What did she find when she opened her purse?

1. Fill in each blank with a suitable adjective from the story above.

   a. Besides postcards, the shop sold _______ magazines.

   b. Susie had made friends with quite _______ people in the hotel.

   c. _______ the rooms in the hotel had writing tables.

   d. Susie could not find _______ money in her purse to buy stamps.

   e. A kind waiter offered her _______ coins.

2. Circle the correct adjective to complete each sentence.

   a. Weren't there (any / all) letters for me today?

   b. I don't want (several / any) cake, thank you.

   c. Tarla is the author of (all / several) cookbooks.

   d. Kiran was so tired after the trip that she slept (any / all) day.

   e. I'm excited because it's only (a few / several) days till my birthday.

Any, **all**, **several** and **a few** are **adjectives of quantity** that can be used before a noun or pronoun to describe the amount or quantity without giving the exact number.

 ISBN 978-93-5103-602-9

Let's Practise

A. Tick the correct **adjective** to complete each sentence.

1. Mum fills the water jug _____ times a day.

   a. some b. several c. a little

2. Dad drove the car _____ day and by evening we reached home.

   a. all b. a few c. many

3. We visited _____ relatives during our holiday.

   a. a little b. none c. a few

4. There weren't _____ scary rides at the theme park.

   a. several b. any c. no

Take Note
The adjective **all** is used before uncountable and plural nouns. The adjective **any** is often used with negatives or in questions. It is also used before uncountable nouns. The adjectives **several** and **a few** are used before plural nouns.

B. Fill in the blanks with **several**, **all**, **any** or **a few**.

Mrs Singh went to Modern Supermarket to buy groceries. On the ground floor there were __________ counters, but only __________ people were shopping. The delivery vans had not yet arrived, so there wasn't __________ fresh stock available. There were only __________ apples left at the fruit counter. __________ the shelves meant for eggs and other poultry products were empty. __________ shelves in the vegetable section were empty too. The manager of the supermarket did not have __________ information about when the supplies would come in.

C. Make sentences with the words given below.

1. all day

   ____

2. a few miles

   ____

3. any money

   ____

4. several times

   ____

 ISBN 978-93-5103-602-9

4.3 Comparison of adjectives

Read the story.

"These seats are really **bad**, Jim," said Julia. "They're **worse** than the ones we got last time."

"I know, they're **the worst** seats I've ever bought," replied Jim. "Those box seats are **the best**."

"These seats are **good**. They're certainly **better** than the earlier ones. Thanks, Jim," said Julia.

Remember!

Comparative adjectives describe someone or something that has **more** of a quality than another. Superlative adjectives describe someone or something that has **most** of a quality.

Do you think Jim and Julia enjoyed the show?

How does Julia describe the seats they sat in at first?

What is Jim's reply?

How does Julia describe the seats they sat in later?

1. Fill in the blanks with suitable adjectives from the box below.

better	good	worst	best

Jim wanted to buy ________ seats for the show. The box seats gave the ________ view of the stage, but they were sold out. He ended up buying seats with the ________ view. Luckily, he was able to exchange the tickets and get ________ seats.

2. Circle the suitable adjective to complete each sentence.

   a. Sana is a (better / best) singer than Veena.

   b. This is the (worse / worst) storm we've had for years.

   c. Sunita is a (good / better) swimmer, but her sister is the (better / best) swimmer in the school.

   d. Due to (bad / worst) weather, the flight was cancelled.

Some adjectives change their form completely in the **comparative** and **superlative**.

 ISBN 978-93-5103-602-9

Here are some ways in which adjectives form their comparatives and superlatives.

Adjectives that add **-er** and **-est**

Positive	Comparative	Superlative
dark	darker	darkest
dirty	dirtier	dirtiest
fine	finer	finest
narrow	narrower	narrowest
sad	sadder	saddest
simple	simpler	simplest

Adjectives that use **more** and **most**

Positive	Comparative	Superlative
charming	more charming	most charming
delicious	more delicious	most delicious
famous	more famous	most famous
generous	more generous	most generous
intelligent	more intelligent	most intelligent
valuable	more valuable	most valuable

Adjectives that change their form completely

Positive	Comparative	Superlative
bad	worse	worst
far	further/farther	furthest/farthest
good	better	best
little	less	least
many	more	most
much	more	most

  ISBN 978-93-5103-602-9

Let's Practise

A. Write the **positive** form of each underlined **adjective** in the blank.

1. Yesterday was the wettest day of the year. ____________
2. Mary is the slimmest in the class. ____________
3. Who has the largest feet? ____________
4. That was the nicest birthday party I've ever had. ____________
5. This pink car is faster than that blue one. ____________

B. Fill in each blank with the correct form of the **adjective** given in the brackets.

1. That's the ____________ story I've ever heard. (strange)
2. Grandfather is the ____________ person in our family. (wise)
3. My brother's desk is ____________ than mine. (tidy)
4. Which is the ____________ river in the world? (long)
5. Karim is ____________ than Jai. (thin)

C. Fill in each blank with **more** or **most**.

1. Which lesson do you find the ____________ interesting?
2. The Maths exam was ____________ difficult than the English one.
3. Govind's injury was ____________ serious than we had thought it was.
4. The green armchair is ____________ comfortable than the blue one.
5. Which of today's tasks is the ____________ important?
6. Of all the songs I know, this one has the ____________ ridiculous words.
7. You got a ____________ generous helping of fries than I did.
8. In which country do you find the ____________ poisonous snakes?

Remember!
In the case of longer adjectives, we use **more** to express the comparative and **most** to express the superlative. We usually use **the** before a superlative adjective.

D. Fill in each blank with the correct form of the **adjective** given in the brackets.

1. Which planet is ____________ (far) from the sun?
2. This laptop is ____________ (good) than that one.
3. Sahil had the ____________ (little) homework to do.
4. The cricket team's performance yesterday was the ____________ (bad) I have ever seen.
5. Geeta has collected ____________ (many) stamps than her brother.

 ISBN 978-93-5103-602-9

5 Verbs

Let's Recall

- Doing and being words are called **verbs**.
- We use I **have**, you **have**, he/she/it **has**, we **have** or they **have** when we talk about the present. We use **had** when we talk about the past.
- We use **may** with another verb to give permission, make a request or talk about something that could happen. We use **can** to say that we are able to do something.
- We use **there is** and **there are** to talk about what exists or can be found. We use **there is** with a singular noun and **there are** with a plural noun.
- A **tense** is a form taken by a verb to show the time of an action.
- We use the **simple present tense** to talk about facts and habits and about things as they happen. The **present continuous tense** tells us that something is happening now. We use the verbs **is**, **am** and **are** as helping verbs with the **-ing** form of the main verbs to form the present continuous tense.
- The **simple past tense** tells us about things that happened earlier. The **past continuous tense** tells us that something was happening at a particular time in the past. We use the verbs **was** and **were** as helping verbs with the **-ing** form of the main verbs to form the past continuous tense.
- Most verbs add **-d** or **-ed** to refer to the past. They are called **regular verbs**. Some verbs change their spellings when they refer to the past. They are called **irregular verbs**.
- The **simple future tense** tells us that something is yet to happen. We use the verbs **will** and **shall** as helping verbs with the main verbs to form the simple future tense.

5.1 Revising verbs

1. Complete each sentence with **have** or **has** and a suitable phrase from the box below.

grey hair and glasses	two humps	long tails
a thick coat of white fur	a red cover	

a. Polar bears ____________________.

b. Old Mrs Singh ____________________.

c. Monkeys ____________________.

d. My book ____________________.

e. Some camels ____________________.

Remember!
Has basically means "to own". Sometimes it is used to describe a person or thing, e.g. Neil **has** brown eyes.

 ISBN 978-93-5103-602-9

2. Choose a **verb** from the box that means the same as **has** in each sentence. Write it in the blank.

eats	drinks	owns	takes	gives

a. Ali (has) a laptop and a mobile phone. ________

b. Dad (has) a bath before he goes to bed. ________

c. Mum (has) a glass of orange juice for breakfast. ________

d. Jai just (has) a sandwich for lunch. ________

e. Bina always (has) a party for her birthday. ________

3. Circle the correct word to complete each sentence.

a. It (may / can) rain tomorrow.

b. If the weather's fine, we (can / may) go to the zoo.

c. (May / Can) you swim?

d. You (can / may) play when you've finished the exercise.

e. Dad (may / can) be at home if he is not at work.

4. Fill in each blank with **can** or **may**. Use **may** for permission.

a. You _______ watch television when you've done your homework.

b. I think I _______ smell something burning.

c. Dina _______ sing very well.

d. _______ my mum and dad come to the school concert?

e. _______ you reach the top shelf?

f. Mustafa _______ speak French.

g. Students _______ use calculators during the exam.

h. You _______ leave after the concert is over.

5. Fill in the blanks with **can** or **may** and a verb from the box below.

Remember!
Can and **may** always come before the main verb.

take	touch	swim	borrow	snow	bring

a. I ______________ ten lengths of the pool.

b. You ______________ not ______________ food out of the fridge without asking.

c. ______________ you ______________ your nose with your tongue?

d. Put on warm clothes as it ______________.

e. ______________ I ______________ your mobile phone?

f. Members ______________ two guests to the show.

 ISBN 978-93-5103-602-9

6. Complete each sentence with **There is** or **There are**.

a. __________ a carton of milk in the fridge.

b. __________ two sides to every argument.

c. __________ some questions I'd like to ask you.

d. __________ no paper in the printer.

e. __________ a big spider in the bathtub.

f. __________ no new e-mails in my inbox.

7. Fill in each blank with a suitable present, past or question form of **there is** or **there are**.

a. Did you have a good journey? __________ any snow on the road?

b. __________ enough glasses for everyone at the reception last week.

c. __________ a spare computer in the office that I can use?

d. __________ no trains to Chennai yesterday because of the floods.

e. I tried to help, but __________ nothing I could do.

f. __________ plenty of fruit in the bowl.

g. __________ many people at the theatre last night?

h. __________ lots of food left over after the party.

Take Note

- When talking about the past, we use **there was** or **there were**. In questions we say **is there**, **are there**, **was there** or **were there**.
- Even though "a lot of" is singular and "lots of" is plural, we use **there is** and **there are** to match the noun that comes after "a lot of" or "lots of", e.g. **There are** a lot of **holes** in the road. **There is** lots of **mud** on the road.

8. Fill in the blanks with the correct words from the box below.

there is	is there	there were	there are
was there	are there	there was	

I found three letters in the letter box today. __________ two for Mum and __________ one for Dad.

"__________ one for me?" asked Hamid.

"No," I replied, "__________ nothing for you."

"__________ any letters for me?" called Jamila from the next room.

"No, __________ none for you either," I shouted.

Everyone seemed to be expecting a letter. __________ any other letter I had missed?

  ISBN 978-93-5103-602-9

9. Complete the table with the correct form of the **verbs**.

	Simple present (singular)	**Simple present (plural)**	**Simple past (singular and plural)**
a.	comes	come	
b.		do	did
c.	eats		ate
d.	gets	get	
e.		give	gave
f.	goes		went
g.	puts	put	
h.		say	said
i.	sees		saw
j.	sits	sit	
k.		stand	stood
l.	takes		took

10. Fill in the blanks with the correct form of the **verbs** given in the brackets.

a. I opened the door and there ______ Pia. (stand)

b. Mum ______ it's bedtime, and that we should switch off the lights. (say)

c. I ______ home at four o'clock yesterday. (get)

d. Last night, Dilip ______ his homework as soon as he ______ home. (do, come)

e. Seema was tired so she ______ straight to bed. (go)

f. I ______ the chocolates that you ______ me for my birthday. (eat, give)

g. I once ______ an eclipse of the sun. (see)

h. My sister ______ to the gym every day. (go)

11. Make a sentence with each **verb**. Use it in the form given in the brackets.

a. sing (simple present singular)

____

b. hit (simple present plural)

____

c. find (simple past)

____

 ISBN 978-93-5103-602-9

12. Circle the correct form of the **verb** to complete each sentence below.

a. Rina (is going / was going) to the market yesterday when it started raining.

b. I need to hurry because Jeff and Julia (were waiting / are waiting) for me at the park.

c. Mehak's dog (is sleeping / was sleeping) right now.

d. My teacher (is checking / was checking) the test papers when I walked in.

e. I (was talking / am talking) to my friend when the fire alarm went off.

f. The teacher scolded Vani because she (is sleeping / was sleeping) in class.

13. Rewrite each sentence in the blank below using the **simple future tense**.

Example I went to Gurman's house.

I shall go to Gurman's house.

a. We meet after work at this snack bar.

____

b. Our parents joined us at the mall after some time.

____

c. They visited Grandmother in hospital.

____

d. Mum spoke to the principal about the school trip.

____

e. Jenna performed with Alisha at the show.

____

f. Mansi did her homework before dinner.

____

g. He drove all the way to Agra without a break.

____

h. Tanya prepared all the food.

____

 ISBN 978-93-5103-602-9

5.2 The present participle

Read the story.

Sam **is recycling** some drink cans. He **is putting** them into a bin for special collection.

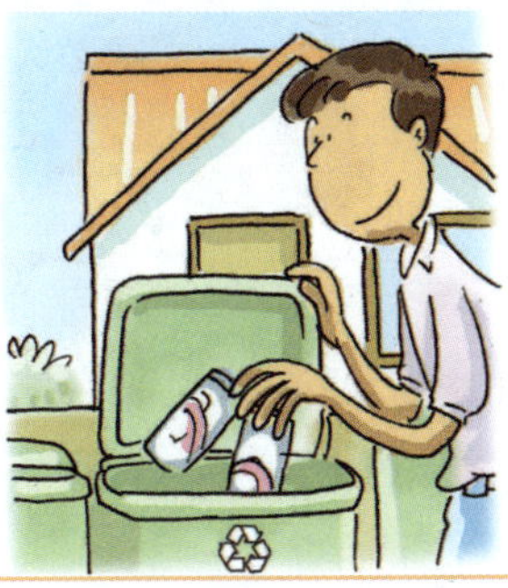

Sam **is switching** on his kettle for a cup of tea. Outside, the wind **is turning** the blades of the windmill.

Sam spends a **relaxing** afternoon, **drinking** his cup of tea and **admiring** his windmill.

Do you think Sam cares for the environment?
How do you know?

What is Sam doing with the drink cans?

What is the wind doing?

What is happening in the last picture?

1. Note the highlighted **-ing** forms in the sentences above. Now fill in each blank with a word from the box.

recycling	caring	using

a. Sam is a __________ person. He is concerned about the environment.

b. He is always __________ paper, cans and bottles.

c. __________ electricity produced by his windmill, Sam saves precious energy.

2. Fill in each blank with the **-ing** form of the verbs given in the brackets.

a. I am __________ a film about dinosaurs. (watch)

b. Will you be __________ Grandmother today? (see)

c. In Geography, we are __________ about the __________ problems in the world. (learn, worry)

d. "Are you __________ here?" "No, I am __________ home." (stay, go)

The **-ing** form of a verb is called the **present participle**. It can be used in the continuous tenses, for example, She **is riding** her bicycle. It can also be used as an adjective, for example, a **shocking** event, a **boring** lesson.

 ISBN 978-93-5103-602-9

Let's Practise

A. Fill in the blanks with the **present participles** of the verbs given in the brackets.

1. Your exam results are rather ________. (disappoint)
2. It's nice to see a lot of ________ faces. (smile)
3. Amit is ________ a game on the computer, ________ to music and ________, all at the same time! (play, listen, eat)
4. We were just ________ to take a rest. (stop)
5. Anushka and Sunil are ________ as usual. (argue)
6. Look, Mum! It is ________ outside. (pour)

B. Circle the **present participles** that are used in the **continuous tenses**, and underline those that are used as **adjectives**.

The Singhs are an interesting family. They came to Delhi from Germany last year, and were renting a flat in Saket. Now they have bought a house in Dwarka and are already living there. They have two charming children, Nimmi, who is attending the local primary school, and Sunny, who is starting at the nursery next month. Nimmi is a promising student and is learning to read and write very quickly, which is very encouraging. Sunny is a mischievous boy, and is always misbehaving. Mrs Singh is a lawyer and is working with a law firm. It is a rewarding job. Mr Singh is writing a book. He stays at home and looks after Sunny. And that is a very demanding job!

Take Note
Present participles can be used without repeating the helping verbs, e.g. Sally was **running** through the park, **listening** to the birds and **feeling** happy.

C. Make a sentence with the **present participles**. Use at least one as a **verb** and one as an **adjective**.

1. sweeping

____

2. exciting

____

3. changing

____

 ISBN 978-93-5103-602-9

5.3 The past participle

Read the story.

Tom was cycling up a steep hill. Mum **had asked** him to collect a parcel from Aunt Mary.

He **had cycled** only halfway up the hill when he felt **tired** and stopped to rest.

When Tom woke up, it **had started** to drizzle, so Tom cycled back home instead.

Do you think Mum was happy when Tom returned home? What do you think she said to him?

Why was Tom cycling up the hill?

When did he stop to rest?

Why did he return home?

1. Note the highlighted **-ed** forms in the story above. Now fill in the blanks with suitable words from the box below.

forced	tired	stopped	decided	determined

a. Tom was a ________ boy and he was sure he could cycle all the way to Aunt Mary's house.

b. He had ________ to take a short cut and cycle up the hill.

c. He had ________ himself to keep cycling even when he felt ________.

d. He had ________ to rest for a while, but fell asleep instead!

2. Fill in each blank with the **-ed** form of the verb(s) given in the brackets.

a. My brother and I had ________ an art competition. (enter)

b. I had ________ a beautiful picture, but my brother had spilt juice on it. (paint)

c. I was ________ because I wouldn't win a prize. (disappoint)

d. The ________ children gathered round the judges to hear the results. (excite)

e. My brother was ________ when he won a prize. He gave it to me because he had ________ my painting. (delight, ruin)

We use the **-ed** form of a verb to talk about actions that happened earlier. When it is used with **has**, **have** or **had**, it is called the **past participle**. Past participles can also be used as adjectives, for example, **cooked** vegetables.

 ISBN 978-93-5103-602-9

The simple past and past participle of irregular verbs may be the same, for example, win/**won**/has **won**, or different, for example, eat/**ate**/has **eaten**.

Let's Practise

A. Fill in the missing **verb forms**.

	Verb	Simple past	Past participle
1.	bite		bitten
2.	break		broken
3.	bring	brought	
4.		cancelled	cancelled
5.	carry	carried	
6.		came	come
7.		cried	cried
8.	do		done
9.	drink	drank	
10.	fall	fell	
11.	feel		felt

	Verb	Simple past	Past participle
12.	find		found
13.		flew	flown
14.		got	got
15.	go		gone
16.	hit		hit
17.	hold		held
18.	let	let	
19.	make	made	
20.	see		seen
21.	sit		sat
22.		swam	swum

B. Fill in each blank with the **past participle** of the verb given in the brackets. Then write **A** if it is an adjective or **V** if it is a verb.

1. I have never ______________ (taste) oysters before. [ ]
2. The ______________ (terrify) children hid in the cellar. [ ]
3. Jane had already ______________ (go) home. [ ]
4. The instructions are rather ______________ (complicate). [ ]
5. Someone has ______________ (drink) all the milk. [ ]
6. We shall reschedule the ______________ (cancel) match. [ ]
7. I swept up the ______________ (fall) leaves. [ ]
8. By the time I got my camera, the birds had ______________ (fly) away. [ ]
9. Dad uses ______________ (dry) herbs in his cooking. [ ]
10. Oh no! Mum's favourite vase is ______________ (break). [ ]

 ISBN 978-93-5103-602-9

5.4 Present perfect tense

Read the story.

Kate **has offered** to teach Ron how to play tennis.

Kate **has beaten** Ron in every game so far, but Ron's game is improving.

Ron **has promised** to teach Kate chess in return. He **has won** many prizes in chess!

Do you think Kate will be able to win a game of chess against Ron? Why?

What has Kate offered to do?

How is Ron doing at tennis?

What has Ron promised Kate?

1. Fill in the blanks with suitable verbs from the story above.

   Kate is a good tennis player. She __________ many prizes at tournaments. She __________ several well-known players. Ron wants to learn tennis and Kate __________ to teach him. Kate doesn't know how to play chess, so Ron __________ to teach her. Soon Ron and Kate will be able to play each other well at tennis and chess.

2. Circle the correct form of the verb to complete each sentence below.

   a. Tina looks so different. She (loses / has lost) a lot of weight!
   b. Vishal can't dance tonight as he (has hurt / have hurt) his ankle.
   c. We (are living / have lived) in Chennai for the past ten years.
   d. I didn't recognise you! You (grow / have grown) a moustache!

We use the **present perfect tense** to talk about an action that happened in the past but still affects the present or continues in the present. We form the present perfect tense by using the helping verb **has** or **have** with the past participle of the main verb, for example, Mum, you **have changed** your hairstyle!

 ISBN 978-93-5103-602-9

Let's Practise

A. Complete the letter with **verbs** from the box below.

have heard	have located	have set
have sworn	have learnt	

Dear Nina,

I ________ out on an exciting journey with my brother to find the mysterious island of Chocola. I'm sure you ________ the legends about the island. The stories about the orange-centred flowers and the mint-flavoured chocolate fruit that grow on Chocola are known all over the world. I ________ to be the first to discover the fiery chocolate-fudge volcano. Did you know its molten centre turns cool once a year? Now that I ________ this fact, I long to find the island!

I will write to you again when we ________ Chocola.

Your friend,

Swati

B. Rewrite each sentence by changing the underlined verbs to the **present perfect tense**.

1. Dad broke the jug.

____

2. Tommy talks to the security guard.

____

3. The sun is rising over the mountains.

____

4. I notice that Lakshmi arrives late every day.

____

5. Amar lost his car keys, so he can't go home now.

____

6. She got good grades in English.

____

 ISBN 978-93-5103-602-9

The present tense has different forms. We use the **simple present tense** to talk about facts and habits, for example, Dad **enjoys** visiting his brother Bobby. We use the **present continuous tense** (**is/am/are** with the present participle) for an activity going on at present, for example, Jessie **is building** a robot. We use the **present perfect tense** (**have/has** with the past participle) to talk about an action that happened in the past, but still affects the present, for example, The thread **has broken** again.

Let's Practise

A. Fill in the missing forms of the **present tense verbs**.

	Verb	Simple present	Present continuous	Present perfect
Example	walk	She walks.	She is walking.	She has walked.
1.	arrive	It arrives.	It ____________.	It ____________.
2.	carry	I carry.	I ____________.	I have carried.
3.	dress	She dresses.	She ____________.	She ____________.
4.	look	They ________.	They ____________.	They ____________.
5.	point	He ________.	He is pointing.	He ____________.
6.	polish	We polish.	We ____________.	We have polished.
7.	read	I ________.	I am reading.	I ____________.
8.	sing	They sing.	They ____________.	They have sung.
9.	wash	He ________.	He is washing.	He ____________.
10.	work	You ________.	You are working.	You ____________.

B. Fill in the blanks with the correct form of the **verb** given in the brackets.

1. If you ______________ that book, may I borrow it? (finish)
2. Joe ______________ a happy tune as he mows the grass. (whistle)
3. Mr Bakshi ______________ his grandchildren very much, so he ______________ to them over the phone every week. (miss, speak)
4. My brother, my sister and I all ______________ the same school. (attend)
5. Chang ______________ to judge the art competition today. (agree)
6. Tanya often ______________ me when I am working. (interrupt)

 ISBN 978-93-5103-602-9

7. Pia always ________ through her homework. That's why she ________ so many mistakes. (hurry, make)
8. When the weather is fine, we sometimes ________ for a long walk in the park. (go)
9. Rajesh ________ twenty years at his current job. (complete)
10. I ________ my Science project right now. (do)
11. You ________ hard all this term. Well done! (work)
12. Dad is cross with me. Perhaps I ________ him. (annoy)

Take Note

- For singular verbs ending in **-ss**, we add **-es** for the simple present and **-ed** for the present perfect, e.g. dress**es**, dress**ed**.
- For singular verbs ending in **-e**, we add **-s** for the simple present and **-d** for the present perfect, e.g. arrive**s**, arrive**d**.
- For singular verbs ending in **-y**, we change **-y** to **-ies** for the simple present and to **-ied** for the present perfect, e.g. carr**ies**, carr**ied**.

C. Circle the correct forms of the **present tense verbs** to complete the story below. The pictures will help you.

Tina (has walked / is walking) along the beach. Suddenly the strong wind (is blowing / blows) her hat off. Tina (sees / has seen) that her hat (is landing / has landed) on Danny's back. Danny (wakes / has woken) up in surprise. Tina (is grabbing / grabs) her hat and (runs / has run) off. Danny (has wondered / wonders) what (happens / is happening). His friends (have laughed / laugh) and tell him what (is happening / has happened).

D. Complete the following sentences.

1. Harleen visits ____.
2. My cousin has taken ____________________________________.
3. Abdul is teaching _____________________________________.
4. The athletes are training ________________________________.
5. They have lost ____.

 ISBN 978-93-5103-602-9

5.5 Past perfect tense

Read the story.

Maya **had started** cooking when the doorbell rang.

Her neighbour Carrie said that the postman **had called** while Maya was at work.

Carrie **had taken** in Maya's parcel because Maya was not at home.

What do you think Maya says to Carrie?

What was Maya doing when the doorbell rang?

What did Carrie say?

What had Carrie done when the postman told her Maya was not at home?

1. Note the highlighted verbs in the story above. Now circle the suitable form of the verb to complete each sentence.
   a. Maya (began / had begun) cooking when Carrie rang the doorbell.
   b. The postman (was leaving / had left) a parcel with Carrie while Maya was at work.
   c. Carrie (been / had been) at home when the postman called.

2. Fill in the blanks with the suitable form of the verbs given in the brackets.

   Yesterday my sister called. She told me that her son Jehan ________ (play) the piano at a concert a few days earlier. The audience ________ (love) his performance so they gave him a standing ovation. He was thrilled to see that everyone ________ (enjoy) his music.

We use the **past perfect tense** to report something that happened in the past before the time we are talking about. We form the past perfect tense by using the helping verb **had** with the past participle of the main verb, for example, Harshit **had** already **spoken** to Sheila before she left for work.

 ISBN 978-93-5103-602-9

Let's Practise

A. Fill in the blanks with the **past perfect tense** of the verbs given in the brackets to complete the sentences.

Example Veena looked at the clock and realised that she had forgotten (forget) to call Dad back.

1. Our school collected clothes and groceries for the people who ________ (lose) their homes in the recent earthquake.
2. I ________ (mean) to go the market yesterday but then some work came up.
3. You didn't tell me you ________ (change) your job.
4. She realised too late that she ________ (take) her sister's laptop bag by mistake!
5. We heard on the news that there ________ (be) a robbery at the bank.
6. Joe noticed that Mum ________ (leave) her bag behind.
7. Madhu did well in her exam because she ________ (study) hard for it.
8. The dogs ________ (begin) barking even before their master reached the gate.
9. Dev took a holiday as soon as he ________ (complete) the project.
10. The two boys rushed to the platform, but the train ________ (go).

B. Rewrite the story correctly in the blanks below, using the **past perfect tense** of the underlined verbs.

Nisha and Alka spoke on the phone. Nisha told Alka that she was going to the theatre the day before to see the play "The Sleeping Beauty". Alka asked Nisha if she enjoys the performance. Nisha replied that although the girl playing the Sleeping Beauty has acted very well in the first half of the play, she did not like her performance in the second half. Alka was confused. Nisha explained to Alka that the actress sleeps throughout the second half!

____

____

____

____

____

____

____

____

 ISBN 978-93-5103-602-9

The past tense has different forms. We use the **simple past tense** to report actions in the past, for example, Mita **visited** her aunt yesterday. We use the **past continuous tense** (**was/were** with the present participle) to report an action that continued for some time or to say what was going on when a certain thing happened, for example, Mita **was visiting** her aunt when the floods occurred. We use the **past perfect tense** (**had** with the past participle) to report something that happened before the time we are talking about, for example, Mita **had** already **visited** her aunt when the floods occurred.

Let's Practise

A. Fill in the missing forms of the **past tense verbs**.

	Verb	Simple past	Past continuous	Past perfect
Example	act	I acted.	I was acting.	I had acted.
1.	chat	We chatted.	We were ______.	We had ______.
2.	hurry	You ______.	You ____________.	You ____________.
3.	jump	It jumped.	It ____________.	It ____________.
4.	kick	Tim kicked.	Tim ____________.	Tim ____________.
5.	plan	He planned.	He ____________.	He ______ planned.
6.	walk	They ______.	They were ______.	They ______ walked.

B. Fill in the blanks with the correct form of the **verb** given in the brackets.

Mrs D'Souza ____________ (look) out of the window when she ____________ (see) an accident in the street outside. A lady ____________ just ____________ (park) her car on the other side of the road when a van driver, who ____________ (check) his mobile phone instead of watching the road, ____________ (bump) into her parked car. The lady ____________ (get) out of her car to see what ____________ (happen). She ____________ (notice) immediately that the front of the van ____________ (damage) the rear of her car. By then Mrs D'Souza ____________ (come) out and she ____________ (offer) to be a witness. The van driver ____________ (admit) his mistake and ____________ (apologise). The two drivers ____________ (exchange) addresses and the van driver ____________ (drive) off.

 ISBN 978-93-5103-602-9

C. Identify the **tense** of each underlined verb form. In the brackets, write **SP** (simple past), **PC** (past continuous) or **PP** (past perfect).

1. I bought two loaves of bread from the shop. [ ]
2. George had already watered his plants when it began to rain. [ ]
3. We met at the bus stop and set off for the party together. [ ]
4. The baby was crying all night. [ ]
5. I suddenly remembered that I had locked the dog out! [ ]

D. Circle the suitable form of the **verb** to complete each sentence.

1. Dad was always (has lost / lose / losing) his keys, so we bought him a special pouch to keep them in.
2. I (go / have gone / went) to school early today.
3. We (finish / were finishing / had finished) lunch by the time Dad came home.
4. James (win / won / was winning) a prize in the art competition yesterday.

E. Circle the correct forms of the **past tense verbs** to complete the story below. The pictures will help you.

Ellen and Susan (had chatted / were chatting) with each other. Ellen (told / had told) Susan about a barbecue she and her husband Jack (was attending / had attended) the week before. The husbands (had made / made) the burgers while their wives (had laid / were laying) the table. Susan (laughed / had laughed) as she told Ellen how her husband Frank (was burning / had burnt) his tongue while eating a burger straight from the grill!

 ISBN 978-93-5103-602-9

5.6 Future continuous tense

Read the story.

Tomorrow is the class picnic. My class **will be going** to the amusement park.

Everyone **will be coming** to school in their best clothes tomorrow. No uniforms!

Mary **will be wearing** her new outfit and Sam **will be wearing** his favourite red shorts.

Do you think the children enjoy not wearing uniforms to school?

What will happen on the day of the picnic?

How will the children come to school that day?

What will Mary and Sam wear?

1. Read the story and look at the pictures again. Now match the columns.

a.	The class •	• i.	will be wearing her new green top.
b.	Everyone •	• ii.	will be going on a picnic tomorrow.
c.	Mary •	• iii.	will be wearing red-checked shorts.
d.	Sam •	• iv.	will be coming to school in their best clothes.

2. Fill in each blank with the correct form of the verb given in the brackets to complete the sentence.

   a. This time next week Tania ______________ (surf) in Australia.

   b. Look for me when you reach the café. I ______________ (carry) a red bag.

   c. Get off the bus at Central Market. I ______________ (wait) at the bus stop.

   d. They ______________ (live) in Agra for the next year.

We use the **future continuous tense** to talk about planned activities and happenings. We form the future continuous by using **will** or **shall** with **be** and the present participle of the main verb, for example, We **shall be going** for a film tomorrow.

 ISBN 978-93-5103-602-9

Let's Practise

A. Circle the verbs in the **future continuous tense** to complete the story below.

Neal asked Dad, "Who (will be meeting / will meet) us at the airport when we arrive?"

"The hotel (sends / will be sending) a driver to pick us up," Dad replied.

"How shall we recognise him?" asked Neal anxiously.

"He (will wear / will be wearing) the hotel uniform," said Dad.

Neal was still worried. He asked, "What if we don't recognise the uniform?"

Dad smiled at Neal and said, "He (will be holding / is holding) a board with our names on it."

"What if he stands at the back and we can't spot him?" asked Neal.

Dad began to laugh and said, "Don't worry. I (call / shall be calling) him as soon as we land."

Finally satisfied, Neal looked out of the aeroplane window to admire the view.

B. Write five sentences about your favourite festival using the **future continuous tense**. The verbs in the box will help you.

will be wearing	shall be eating	will be making
will be celebrating	shall be visiting	

___

___

___

___

___

___

___

___

___

___

 ISBN 978-93-5103-602-9

5.7 Future perfect tense

Read the story.

Do you think the boy likes bread? Why?

What will happen on 1 October?

What will Dad have done by then?

What does the boy wonder?

1. Note the highlighted words in the story above. Now fill in the blanks below with suitable forms of the verbs given in the brackets.

   "Jeremy, by Christmas this year I ____________ (retire)," said Dad.

   "Wow!" said Jeremy. "When is your last day?" Dad said, "I ____________ (complete) twenty years on 1 October. By then you ____________ (finish) primary school."

2. Tick the suitable form of the verb to complete each sentence.

   a. My letter ____ by now.

      i. will arrive   ii. will be arriving   iii. will have arrived

   b. My parents ____ in Singapore by the time I go to bed tonight.

      i. will have landed   ii. will land   iii. will be landing

   c. Don't worry, I ____ my lines for play practice by Monday.

      i. shall learn   ii. shall have learnt   iii. shall be learning

---

We use the **future perfect tense** for activities that will be over by a particular time in the future. We form the future perfect by using **will** or **shall** with **have** and the past participle of the main verb, for example, The committee **will have made** their decision by eight o'clock.

 ISBN 978-93-5103-602-9

Let's Practise

A. Fill in the blanks with suitable verbs in the **future perfect tense** from the box below.

will have won	shall have taken	will have learnt	will have flown
shall have redone	shall have changed	will have finished	
will have lost	will have blossomed	will have published	

1. By this time next week, I ____________ all my exams.
2. Rohan hopes he ____________ a few kilograms before school starts again.
3. These birds ____________ away by the time winter sets in.
4. Swati ____________ some Vietnamese before she goes there for a trip this summer.
5. The next time you visit us, I expect we ____________ the dining room.
6. I guess I ____________ a lot by the time I'm fifty!
7. Do you think you ____________ your Science project by the weekend?
8. Sam is sure he ____________ a few more debating awards before the school year ends.
9. Mr Ghosh says he ____________ his new book of poems by November.
10. The trees ____________ by the end of March.

B. Rewrite the story correctly in the blanks below, using the **future perfect tense** of the underlined verbs.

At school, Sneha is thinking about the tasks that she still needs to do before the family leave for their vacation. "By the time I reach home, Mum <u>will start</u> her packing. I think Dad <u>will be taking</u> out the winter coats by now. I forgot to remind him about the boots, but perhaps he <u>will be remembering</u> before I get back." The teacher suddenly announces, "Students, we shall focus on verbs this month. By the end of the semester you <u>learn</u> all the different tenses." Sneha gulps nervously and thinks, "Oops! I'd better pay attention!"

____

____

____

____

____

____

 ISBN 978-93-5103-602-9

The future tense has different forms. We use the **simple future tense** to talk about plans and things that are going to happen, for example, They **will go** to the park tomorrow. We use the **future continuous tense** (**will/shall** + **be** with the present participle) to talk about planned activities and things that will be happening at a certain point in the future, for example, They **will be going** for a picnic tomorrow. We use the **future perfect tense** (**will/shall** + **have** with the past participle) for activities that will be over by a particular time in the future, for example, They **will have returned** from their picnic by seven o'clock.

Let's Practise

A. Fill in the missing forms of the **future tense verbs**.

	Verb	Simple future	Future continuous	Future perfect
Example	work	You will work.	You will be working.	You will have worked.
1.	brush	She will brush.	She ____________.	She will have ______.
2.	dance	We ______.	We shall be dancing.	We ____________.
3.	eat	I shall eat.	I ____________.	I shall ______ eaten.
4.	listen	They ______.	They ____________.	They will have listened.
5.	read	Sonali ______.	Sonali will be reading.	Sonali ____________.
6.	see	He will see.	He ____________.	He ____________ seen.
7.	talk	They ______.	They will be ______.	They will have talked.
8.	win	Ria ______.	Ria will be ______.	Ria will have won.

B. Each sentence expresses either a decision or plan, or a guess. In the brackets, write **D** (decision or plan) or **G** (guess).

1. Right now my friends **will be lying** on a beach, sunbathing. [ ]
2. I **shall be going** to a new school next year. [ ]
3. They **will bring** their guitars tomorrow. [ ]
4. Joe **will be** quite happy to leave school. [ ]
5. You have a lot to do – we **shall come** and help you. [ ]
6. We're too late – the bus **will have left** by now! [ ]
7. Aditi **will visit** her mother next week. [ ]
8. We **shall be attending** the lecture this evening. [ ]

Take Note

- We use the simple future and future continuous to state plans and decisions, or make guesses about the future or the present.
- We use the future perfect to guess what has happened or will have happened by a certain time.

 ISBN 978-93-5103-602-9

C. Fill in the blanks with the correct form of the **verbs** given in the brackets.

I shall be __________ (take) my vacation in July this year. I think I __________ (go) to Sri Lanka. I __________ just__________ (move) house at the end of June, so I __________ be __________ (need) a rest. Sri Lanka __________ (be) very relaxing. I __________ (visit) some beautiful cities and I __________ (enjoy) the warm weather. I know you __________ (finish) your project by then, so would you like to come with me? I __________ be __________ (wait) for your answer. I __________ be __________ (book) a room at the Atlanta Hotel, so let me know if I should book one for you as well.

D. Circle the correct forms of the **future tense verbs** to complete the story below. The pictures will help you.

Mr Hill called the principal of the school and said, "I (shall be coming / will come) to your school today. I (shall have selected / shall select) students for the annual dance festival. They (will be dancing / will have danced) on the opening day." After seeing the children dance, he announced, "All of you (will perform / shall be performing) in my show! By this time next month, you (will learn / will have learnt) all the basic steps. After that, it's just practice." Susie showed Mr Hill around the school. He saw pictures of the children performing different dances. Susie said, "We (shall have learnt / will learn) all these dance forms by the time we leave school."

 ISBN 978-93-5103-602-9

5.8 Could, should, might, must

Read the story.

Harry asked Jenny to get him a book from the top shelf. She **could** hear him, but was too busy to help.

Jenny knew she **should** help him, but she just told him to use the stool instead.

Just then, Mum walked in. "Harry! You **might** fall! You **must** get down at once!" she exclaimed.

Do you think Jenny is sorry she didn't help Harry?
How does she feel now?

Why didn't Jenny help Harry?

What did Jenny know she should do?

What did Mum tell Harry?

1. Fill in each blank with a suitable verb from the story above.
   a. Harry was too short, so he ______ not reach the top shelf.
   b. Mum was worried that Harry ______ hurt himself.
   c. Mum said Jenny ______ always help her little brother.
   d. Mum told Harry he ______ never try climbing up like that again.

2. Fill in each blank with **could**, **should**, **might** or **must**.
   a. I ______ hear a bird singing nearby.
   b. You ______ always tell the truth.
   c. I ______ hurry or I'll miss my train.
   d. Hold on to the rail or you ______ slip.

Could, **should**, **might** and **must** are helping verbs. **Could** is used as the simple past of **can** to express ability. We also use **could** for making suggestions. We use **should** for giving advice and to talk about expected happenings. We use **might** for warnings or guesses about things that haven't happened yet. **Might** is also used like **may** for possibilities. We use **must** to talk about things that we have to do. **Must** is also used for saying what is probable or likely.

 ISBN 978-93-5103-602-9

Let's Practise

A. Circle the correct **helping verb** to complete each sentence.

1. I (might / should) play tennis this evening.
2. We (should / could) all eat healthy food.
3. This form (must / might) be signed by your mother.
4. We (could / should) see a ship on the horizon.
5. The cake (should / can) be baked by now.
6. Run fast or you (might / must) miss the train!

B. Complete the caption for each picture, using the **helping verb** given.

1. **might**

Come away from the edge of the cliff! You ____________________

____.

2. **must**

Why is that little girl crying? She ____________________

____.

3. **could**

What shall we do today? We ____________________

____.

4. **should**

Oh dear, someone has dropped their wallet! Perhaps I _____

____.

 ISBN 978-93-5103-602-9

6 Adverbs

Let's Recall

- Just as adjectives tell us more about nouns, **adverbs** tell us more about verbs.
- Adverbs that tell us how an action is done are called **adverbs of manner**. They answer the question "How?". They usually come after the verb.
- Adverbs that tell us the place of action are called **adverbs of place**. They answer the question "Where?". They usually come after the verb.
- Adverbs that tell us the time of action are called **adverbs of time**. They answer the question "When?". Sometimes they are used after a noun, e.g. the flat **above**.

6.1 Revising adverbs

1. Fill in each blank by changing the adjective given in the brackets to an **adverb of manner**.

   a. Are you sitting ___________? (comfortable)

   b. Susan writes very ___________. (neat)

   c. John was whistling ___________. (gay)

   d. The man spoke to me ___________. (rude)

   e. Cinderella's clothes changed ___________. (magic)

   f. Hold the baby very ___________. (gentle)

   g. Dad's health is improving ___________. (gradual)

   h. The key fitted ___________ into the lock. (easy)

   i. The children were treated ___________ by their stepmother. (cruel)

   j. Anne tiptoed ___________ up the stairs. (careful)

Remember!

- Most adverbs of manner are formed by adding **-ly** to an adjective, e.g. polite**ly**, sad**ly**, beautiful**ly**.
- For adjectives ending in **-y**, we change **-y** to **-i** before adding **-ly**, e.g. nois**ily**.
- For adjectives ending in **-le**, we lose **-e** before adding **-ly**, e.g. simp**ly**.
- For adjectives ending in **-ic**, we add **-al** before **-ly**, e.g. comic**ally**.

2. Replace the underlined words with an **adverb of manner** from the box below. Rewrite the sentence.

strongly	silently	easily	nicely	bravely

   a. She ran <u>without any fear</u> into the burning house.

   ____

   b. Harish slipped into class <u>without making any noise</u>.

   ____

 ISBN 978-93-5103-602-9

c. The horse jumped over the fence <u>without difficulty</u>.

____

d. That dress fits you <u>very well</u>.

____

e. The wind blew <u>with a lot of force</u>.

____

3. Fill in each blank with **here**, **there**, **above**, **below**, **near** or **behind**.

a. The Kumars live on the floor ________.

b. ________ comes the bus!

c. What are you doing up ________ on the wall?

d. The balloons floated high ________.

e. ________ is your ring, on the table.

f. In a flash, the young man jumped into the sea ________ to save the drowning child.

g. Come ________ and look at what I have found.

h. Put the bowl down over ________.

i. The dog scares away anyone who comes ________.

j. Please don't leave me ________ when you go for the flower show.

4. Circle the correct **adverb of time** to complete each sentence.

a. We are packing up (today / yesterday) to catch the evening train.

b. The Kapoor family will be moving into their new house (yesterday / tomorrow).

c. (Yesterday / Tomorrow), late at night, there was a huge thunderstorm.

d. Come to my office (today / yesterday) at 6 o'clock.

e. The swimming competition will finish at 5.30 p.m. (yesterday / tomorrow).

f. The forecast says it will be windy (yesterday / tomorrow).

g. It was my birthday (today / yesterday).

h. The weather is lovely (yesterday / today). Shall we go for a walk?

Think & Share Get into groups and play a game of Dumb Charades with adverbs. Each group has a list of adverbs of manner, place and time. One member of each group has to act out the adverb while the other group tries to guess it, for example, **slowly**, **tomorrow** and **here**.

 ISBN 978-93-5103-602-9

6.2 Adverbs of place

Read the story.

Mr Smith was **outside** in the garden. Weeds were growing **everywhere**. As he bent **down**, he felt a pain in his back.

He sat **down** to rest, but did not notice the dark clouds gathering in the sky.

Suddenly it began to rain. "Oh dear! I can't stay here. I'd better get **inside**!" he cried.

Why do you think Mr Smith was weeding the garden?

Where was Mr Smith working?

What did he not notice?

Where did Mr Smith run when it began to rain?

1. Note the highlighted adverbs in the story above. Now fill in each blank with an adverb that is opposite in meaning to the underlined adverb.
   a. Mr Smith was working outside. He ran ________ to shelter from the rain.
   b. He bent down to clear the weeds. When he stood ________, his back began to hurt.
   c. He looked everywhere for his walking stick, but he couldn't find it ________.

2. Fill in each blank with an adverb from the box below.

anywhere	outside	everywhere	inside

   a. I heard a noise ______________ in the street.
   b. Dad can't find his glasses ______________.
   c. We carried the shopping ______________.
   d. Books were lying ______________ around the house.

Adverbs of place, such as **down**, **up**, **outside**, **inside**, **anywhere** and **everywhere**, tell us where an action takes place. They answer the question "Where?".

 ISBN 978-93-5103-602-9

Let's Practise

A. Fill in each blank with an **adverb of place** from the box below.

away	in	up	back	anywhere	somewhere

1. I can't find my ring ______________.
2. Our neighbours' house is empty. They have gone ______________.
3. Mum comes ______________ from her office at about six o'clock.
4. Dad picked Lily ______________ and put her on his shoulders.
5. I went to Jai's house but he was not ______________.
6. I've left my phone ______________ and I can't remember where.

B. Fill in each blank with a suitable **adverb** from the box below. You can use them more than once.

back	down	here	in	out	there	up

1. ______________ walked the headmaster.
2. ______________ he went to the sleepy village from where he had come.
3. ______________ came the sun and dried up the rain.
4. ______________ comes the postman.
5. ______________ came the rain in torrents.
6. ______________ went everyone's umbrella.
7. ______________ is the book you wanted.
8. ______________ goes the bus! I've missed it!

C. Make a sentence with each **adverb**.

1. everywhere

____

2. somewhere

____

3. anywhere

____

4. inside

____

5. down

____

 ISBN 978-93-5103-602-9

6.3 Adverbs of time

Remember!
Use the right tense with time adverbs like **yesterday, today** and **tomorrow**, e.g. We **arrived** yesterday, we **are staying** here today, and we **shall leave** tomorrow.

Read the story.

What do you think happened next?

When did Maggie first wake up?

What did she say when she saw the birds singing?

What happened after she got back into bed?

1. Note the highlighted adverbs in the story above. Now match the two columns.

a.	Maggie woke up •	• i.	soon.
b.	The birds are singing •	• ii.	late.
c.	Maggie fell asleep •	• iii.	now.
d.	Maggie got up •	• iv.	early.

2. Circle the adverbs that show when something happens.
   a. Mr Mishra comes home from work late on Fridays.
   b. Homi was woken early by the ringing of the alarm clock.
   c. I hope the postman comes soon.
   d. You must go home now.
   e. Suman worked late to finish her project.
   f. She soon realised what the problem was.
   g. Things were easier then.
   h. Now we know the truth.

Adverbs of time, such as **early, soon, late, then** and **now**, tell us when an action takes place. They answer the question "When?".

 ISBN 978-93-5103-602-9

Let's Practise

A. Fill in each blank with a suitable **adverb of time** from the box below.

late	tomorrow	yesterday	early	now	soon

1. The train arrived __________, so they had time to settle down.
2. I can't come right __________. I'll be with you in ten minutes.
3. The forecast says it will be windy __________.
4. Get ready! We shall be landing __________.
5. It was Salim's birthday __________.
6. We get up __________ on a Sunday.

B. Fill in each blank with **now**, **then** or **soon**.

1. I was only a little child ________.
2. I met her five years ago. She was about twelve ________.
3. I have ________ decided to become a doctor.
4. Where are we going ________?
5. Don't worry, you will ________ make friends.

Take Note

- An adverb of time often comes after a helping verb, e.g. You will **soon** make progress.
- The adverb **then** is often used to say what happened next, e.g. Sue got out of bed. **Then** she made a cup of tea.

C. Replace the underlined words with an **adverb** from the box below. Rewrite each sentence.

tomorrow	now	then	early	soon

1. Your flight is at this moment ready for boarding.

____

2. He is planning to meet Sudha the day after today.

____

3. In a short time it will be too dark to see our way.

____

4. The door opened slowly. What happened afterwards?

____

5. Raghav rushed through breakfast because he wanted to reach school before the usual time.

____

 ISBN 978-93-5103-602-9

6.4 Adverbs of frequency

Read the story.

At Christmas, Peter's family **sometimes** comes to stay with Andy's family.

They **always** give each other Christmas presents. Peter and Andy **often** give each other a book.

This Christmas, they found they had got the same book. "This has **never** happened before!" said Andy.

What do you think Peter and Andy will do now?

When does Peter's family visit Andy's family?

What is Peter and Andy's favourite hobby?
How do you know?

What did Peter and Andy find when they opened their presents?

1. Fill in each blank with a suitable adverb from the story above.
   a. How often does Peter's family visit Andy's family? __________
   b. How often do the families exchange Christmas presents? __________
   c. How often do Peter and Andy give each other a book? __________
   d. How often had they received the same book? __________

2. In each sentence, circle the adverb that tells you how often the action takes place.
   a. Dev never eats meat.
   b. I always check that I have my keys before leaving the house.
   c. Mum sometimes goes to the gym after work.
   d. I often play cricket with my cousins.

Adverbs of frequency, such as **sometimes**, **often**, **never** and **always**, tell us how often an action takes or does not take place. They answer the question "How often?".

 ISBN 978-93-5103-602-9

Let's Practise

A. Rewrite each sentence using the **adverb of frequency** given in the brackets.

1. We have gym on a Monday. (always)

   ____

2. I have been to Disneyland. (never)

   ____

3. I shall think about you. (often)

   ____

4. Even teachers make mistakes. (sometimes)

   ____

5. You should be rude to people. (never)

   ____

Take Note
If the verb is a single word, the adverb of frequency comes before it, e.g. Rina **always** comes early. If the verb has two or more words, the adverb of frequency comes after the first one, e.g. I have **never** met him. In commands **always** and **never** come first, e.g. **Always** tell the truth.

B. Use the adverb **always** or **never** to complete the caption for each picture.

1. 

   ______________________ before crossing the road.

2. 

   ______________________ a lift from a stranger.

3. 

   ______________________ put rubbish in a dustbin.

4. 

   __________ check your change when leaving the counter.

 ISBN 978-93-5103-602-9

6.5 Comparison of adverbs

Read the story.

Mr Harris is checking the children's lunch boxes to make sure they are eating **healthily**.

He is delighted to see that the twins are eating **more healthily** than other children.

"Sue and Emma eat the **most healthily** in the whole class," says Mr Harris.

How do you think Sue and Emma feel?

Why was Mr Harris checking the lunch boxes?

How did he know the twins were eating more healthily?

What did he tell the class?

1. Note the highlighted adverbs in the story above. Now fill in the blanks with words from the box.

slowly	carefully	most quickly	more slowly	quickly

The twins' mother plans their lunch ___________ every day. She tells them to chew the food ___________ while eating. Sue chews her food ___________ than Emma, who likes to gobble it down ___________. Emma's friend Asma eats the ___________ of all. She finishes her lunch in just five minutes!

2. Tick the correct adverb to complete each sentence.

a. Hari works _____ than Prakash.

i. hard ii. harder iii. hardest

b. Of all the wild animals, the cheetah runs the _____.

i. fast ii. faster iii. fastest

c. Jim got the _____ to the correct answer.

i. near ii. nearer iii. nearest

Like adjectives, adverbs have a comparative and a superlative form. We form the **comparative** and **superlative** of adverbs using **more** and **most**. A few adverbs have comparative and superlative forms ending in **-er** and **-est**.

 ISBN 978-93-5103-602-9

Some adverbs have irregular comparatives and superlatives. Given below is a table of **irregular adverbs**.

Positive	Comparative	Superlative
badly	worse	worst
far	further	furthest
little	less	least
much	more	most
well	better	best

Let's Practise

A. Fill in the **comparative** form of each **adverb** given in the brackets.

1. Your praise matters __________ to me than anything else. (much)
2. Mita dances __________ than Pippa. (well)
3. The second band performed __________ than the first. (badly)
4. It rains __________ in the east than in the west. (little)
5. They rowed __________ down the river on the second day of their holiday. (far)

B. Fill in the **superlative** form of each **adverb** given in the brackets.

1. Susan is the ______________ married of all our children. (happily)
2. Which planet travels the ______________ round the sun? (fast)
3. Which district was the ______________ affected by the earthquake? (badly)
4. Which method works the ______________? (efficient)
5. Which of us is the ______________ dressed today? (smartly)

Take Note
The is often used before the superlative, e.g. Which bird sings **the** most sweetly?

C. Fill in each blank with **more** or **the most**.

1. Let's see which of you can do this sum ________ quickly.
2. After my holiday in France, I spoke French ________ fluently.
3. You must behave ________ responsibly in future.
4. Thanks to satellites, weather can be forecast ________ accurately than ever before.
5. That was ________ amusingly written book I've read for quite a while.

 ISBN 978-93-5103-602-9

Review 2

1. Tick the correct **adjective of quantity** to complete each sentence.

   a. Is there _____ water left in the flask?

   i. any ii. all iii. few

   b. Mira bought gifts for _____ her friends.

   i. little ii. any iii. all

   c. Please do not put _____ sugar in my coffee.

   i. some ii. a few iii. any

   d. _____ buildings were damaged in the earthquake.

   i. several ii. much iii. any

   e. May I have _____ sheets of paper?

   i. little ii. a few iii. few

2. Fill in each blank with the correct **comparative** or **superlative** form of the **adjective** given in the brackets.

   a. Are orchids ____________ than roses? (beautiful)

   b. This is the ____________ way I know to peel potatoes. (quick)

   c. Jim wrote the ____________ composition of all. (interesting)

   d. This is the ____________ part of the river. (shallow)

   e. Is there a ____________ bed than this one? (comfortable)

   f. Hazel has ____________ handwriting than I have. (neat)

3. Fill in the blanks with the **simple present**, the **present continuous** or the **present perfect** form of the **verb** given in the brackets.

   Example Lisa is crying because she has lost her doll. (lose)

   a. Dave ____________ his driving test, so he now drives everywhere. (pass)

   b. Mike wants a car, so he ____________ up to buy one. (save)

   c. I knitted my sister a sweater and she ____________ it today. (wear)

   d. Nocturnal animals are animals that ____________ at night. (hunt)

   e. The sea ____________ down since this morning. (calm)

   f. Jane is coming to tea, so I ____________ already ____________ a cake. (bake)

 ISBN 978-93-5103-602-9

4. Fill in the blanks with the **simple past**, the **past continuous** or the **past perfect** form of the **verbs** in the box below. Choose a pair of suitable verbs for each sentence.

cause	cough	finish	get	go	injure	know
limp	move	need	ring	return	stop	throw

Example I was getting into the car when my mobile phone rang.

a. Jerry ____________ because he ____________ his ankle.

b. No one ____________ what ____________ the accident.

c. We ____________ a larger flat, so we ____________ house.

d. I ____________ to the doctor because I ____________ a lot.

e. The train ____________ because someone ____________ rubbish on the track.

f. Chetan ____________ his meal before his parents ____________.

5. Fill in the blanks with the **simple future**, the **future continuous** or the **future perfect** form of the **verbs** given in the brackets.

Remember!
We use **shall** with **I** and **we** in the future tenses.

I am so pleased that you ____________ (come) with me to Mussoorie in May. It ____________ (be) fun planning our journey. As I said, we ____________ (take) a plane to Dehradun and we ____________ (visit) Mussoorie, Dhanaulti and Chamba, driving a hired car. I hope I ____________ (hear) from the hire company by Friday. I ____________ (do) most of the driving, but ____________ (appreciate) your help from time to time. We ____________ (stay) three nights in each place.

6. Circle the correct **helping verb** to complete each sentence.

a. To keep the beach clean, we (should / may) dispose of our trash in dustbins.

b. This song (must / should) win the award this year.

c. You (can / must) study hard if you want to do well in your exam.

d. I'm going to Singapore next month, so I (must / might) meet you.

e. How (would / could) you be so careless? That watch was your grandfather's!

f. (Can / May) I leave before the end of the lesson, Sir?

g. Hina (would / could) do somersaults from a very early age.

h. Cases of infectious illness (may / must) be reported to the authorities.

 ISBN 978-93-5103-602-9

7. Fill in the blanks with **could**, **should**, **might** or **must**. You may use some verbs more than once.

It was time to go to school, but Kumar _______ not find his watch anywhere. He thought it _______ be in the bathroom, but no, it wasn't there.

"_______ it be in the pocket of your trousers?" asked his sister Ruby. He felt in both pockets, but it wasn't there.

"You _______ be more careful with your belongings," said Ruby. "You _______ forget your head one day!"

"You _______ help me instead of making jokes," said Kumar. His sister thought for a minute. "You were wearing it last night," she said, "so it _______ be in the house somewhere."

"There it is!" exclaimed Kumar. And there it was, tucked away behind the table lamp on his desk.

8. Fill in the blanks with the **present** or **past participle** form of the **verbs** given in the brackets.

a. We have just had a very ____________ journey. (tire)

b. The bus was full of ____________ children. (excite)

c. Lemonade is a ____________ drink. (refresh)

d. Alok told me some very ____________ news. (interest)

e. We are always ____________ to hear from ____________ customers. (please, satisfy)

9. Underline the **adverb** in each sentence. Tick the correct box to indicate if it shows **place**, **time** or **frequency**.

	Place	Time	Frequency
a. We sat outside on the lawn.	☐	☐	☐
b. Never leave the house without locking the door.	☐	☐	☐
c. The ship left port and soon we were on the high seas.	☐	☐	☐
d. Shruti was always the first to arrive.	☐	☐	☐
e. Jai woke up early to finish his homework.	☐	☐	☐
f. We often eat meals in the garden.	☐	☐	☐
g. Come inside for tea.	☐	☐	☐
h. You can sometimes hear the cuckoo in these woods.	☐	☐	☐

 ISBN 978-93-5103-602-9

10. Fill in each blank with the **comparative** or **superlative** form of the **adverb** given in the brackets.

a. Which planet lies the ___________ from the sun in the solar system? (far)

b. This is the ___________ crafted piece of jewellery I've ever seen. (finely)

c. Which city was the ___________ affected by the recent flood? (badly)

d. Of all our family, Dad minded the cold British climate the ___________. (little)

e. After doing the course, I can speak Spanish ___________. (fluently)

f. Which film did you enjoy the ___________? (much)

Spot the Error

11. There is a mistake in each sentence. Underline it and rewrite the sentence correctly in the blank below.

a. This is the more beautiful dress I have ever seen.

____

b. Shirin looked for her watch but could not find it somewhere.

____

c. Karan sings better then Kanika.

____

d. The stadium was full of exciting spectators.

____

e. I was finished my homework when the postman knocked.

____

f. Rohit has won many trophies when he was at the sports academy.

____

g. Sonal was disappointing because she had lost the game.

____

h. The children go to school by the bus.

____

i. Vineet must swim when he was only two.

____

j. By this time next month Smita will had completed her project.

____

ISBN 978-93-5103-602-9

7 Prepositions

Let's Recall

- **Prepositions** show a connection between people and things. A preposition is always followed by a noun or a pronoun.
- A preposition that tells us the position of one thing or person in relation to another is called a **preposition of place**.
- A preposition that connects a happening with a point in time to tell us when something happens is called a **preposition of time**.

7.1 Revising prepositions

1. Fill in each blank with **through**, **around**, **across** or **to**.

   a. They dug a deep moat __________ the castle.

   b. Dilip kindly helped the old lady __________ the road.

   c. I remember my first visit __________ Italy.

   d. We walked __________ the forest to the other side.

Take Note
A preposition always has an object. Its object is the noun or pronoun that follows it.

2. Fill in the blanks with **at**, **on** or **in**.

   The Roshan family will be going for their vacation __________ August. Their daughter Simran will be back from boarding school __________ 10 August. Her train arrives __________ ten o'clock. They plan to leave early __________ the morning the next day.

3. Look at each underlined **preposition**. Tick the correct box to indicate if it shows **place** or **time**.

	Place	Time
a. We played football <u>after</u> tea.	☐	☐
b. I sat <u>between</u> Tanya and Natasha.	☐	☐
c. We took the dog <u>to</u> the vet.	☐	☐
d. I went camping <u>during</u> my vacation.	☐	☐
e. I need to change <u>before</u> the gym class.	☐	☐
f. The train went <u>through</u> a long tunnel.	☐	☐

 ISBN 978-93-5103-602-9

7.2 More about prepositions

Read the story.

Who do you think will come to help?

Who was walking with Fred through the woods?

Where did they see Anna?

What did Fred and Susie do?

1. Fill in each blank with a suitable preposition from the story above.
   a. Fred was taking a walk ______ Susie.
   b. They were walking ______ the path.
   c. Fred ran back ______ the track to get help.

2. Circle the correct preposition to complete each sentence.
   a. Sheila sat (to / beside) me on the front seat.
   b. The monkey climbed (up / with) the tree and perched on the topmost branch.
   c. The rabbit suddenly disappeared (down / up) a hole.
   d. Mary has gone to the market (to / with) her mother.

Prepositions such as **up**, **down**, **to** and **beside** are used to indicate the position or direction of something. The preposition **with** is used in descriptions and to show that people and things are together.

 ISBN 978-93-5103-602-9

Let's Practise

A. Fill in each blank with a **preposition** from the box below.

up	beside	down	to	besides	with

1. Will you come to see the film _______ me?
2. The torch slipped from her hand and went clattering _______ the stairs.
3. The shopkeeper spoke _______ Mum for a long time.
4. Farah sat down on the bench _______ Kim.
5. _______ Maths, I have English and History for homework.
6. We had to climb _______ a steep hill to reach the guest house.

Take Note

Besides is a different preposition meaning "as well as", e.g. **Besides** her teaching job, Mum looks after the family.

B. Fill in the blanks in the story with suitable **prepositions**.

It was a pleasant day, so old Mr Joshi went for a long walk. He took the path that went _______ the hill to the lake below. There was a railing all _______ the lake. Mr Joshi sat _______ a wooden bench near the railing and looked out at the lake. A boat _______ a white sail moved slowly _______ the lake. Mr Joshi sat watching, till it was time to go home.

C. Look at each underlined word. Tick the correct box to indicate if it is a **preposition** or an **adverb**.

	Preposition	Adverb
1. I went down to see what was happening.	☐	☐
2. Nina ran down the path to the beach.	☐	☐
3. We walked around, doing nothing much.	☐	☐
4. The girls all sat around the campfire.	☐	☐
5. I can hear footsteps coming up the stairs.	☐	☐
6. Dad asked Jo to hold the rope tightly and climb up.	☐	☐

Take Note

These short direction words can be prepositions or adverbs. A preposition has an object, but an adverb doesn't, e.g. I walked **down** [preposition] the stairs.
I reached the stairs and walked **down** [adverb].

 ISBN 978-93-5103-602-9

8 Conjunctions

Let's Recall

- Words such as **and, or, but, because, so** and **though** help to join words, groups of words or sentences together. They are called **conjunctions**.
- Conjunctions that join sentences introduce the idea that is in the second sentence. **But** often introduces an opposite idea (for example, It looks complicated **but** it's very simple), and **because** introduces a reason for what we say in the first sentence (for example, Sally can't come **because** she is ill).

8.1 Revising conjunctions

1. Fill in each blank with a **conjunction** from the box below.

because	but	or	and	so	though

a. My sisters are called Asma ____________ Layla.

b. Is the lift going up ____________ down?

c. The plant is attractive to look at ____________ very poisonous.

d. Everyone liked the new teacher ____________ she was friendly.

e. ____________ it was raining, she decided to walk.

f. Mala had forgotten her purse, ____________ she went back home.

Take Note

So and **because** both deal with the reason for something. **Because** introduces the reason, e.g. I went to the doctor [why?] **because** I was ill. **So** introduces the reaction, e.g. I was ill, **so** [that was the reason why] I went to the doctor.

2. Join each pair of sentences with a **conjunction**. Write the new sentence below.

a. I ought to tidy my desk. I'm too lazy.

____

b. He didn't go swimming today. He had a cold.

____

c. She had a nasty cough. She went to the doctor.

____

d. Mrs Rao plans to retire next year. She's only 52.

____

 ISBN 978-93-5103-602-9

8.2 More about conjunctions

Read the story.

Tim was feeling nervous **when** he went to the dentist, **although** Mum had told him not to worry.

Dr Brown checked Tim's teeth **while** his assistant held Tim's head. Tim lay still **until** they had finished.

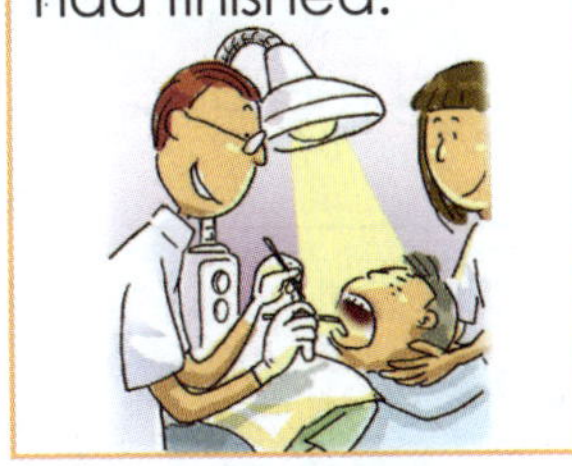

"Your teeth are fine. **If** you want healthy teeth, you must come to me regularly," said Dr Brown.

Have you ever been to a dentist? How did you feel?

When did Tim feel nervous?

How long did Tim lie still in the chair?

What did the doctor tell Tim?

1. Fill in the blanks with conjunctions from the box below.

when	if	until	while	although

"Sit down, Tim," said Dr Brown. Tim sat down and tried to stay calm, __________ his heart was beating fast. Dr Brown said, "Keep your mouth open __________ I tell you to close it." Tim was worried. "__________ I have a bad tooth," he wondered, "will Dr Brown pull it out?" Dr Brown checked his teeth __________ his assistant talked kindly to him. "Your teeth are fine, Tim," he said. Tim breathed a deep sigh of relief __________ he heard this.

2. Circle the correct conjunction to complete each sentence.

a. Fran went out for a walk (until / although) it was raining.

b. I learnt Italian (if / while) I was on holiday in Italy.

c. You will not get supper (when / until) you wash your hands.

d. He does his homework (when / until) he gets home from school.

e. The car will not break down (if / when) it is serviced regularly.

f. Please wash the dishes (when / while) I get the groceries.

The words **when, if, until, while** and **although** are conjunctions. They are used to join sentences.

 ISBN 978-93-5103-602-9

Let's Practise

A. Fill in each blank with a suitable **conjunction** from the box. You may use some conjunctions more than once.

although	if	until	when	while

1. ___________ it was quite warm, the wind made us feel cold.
2. Mum likes to sing ___________ she is working in the kitchen.
3. ___________ you arrive at the station, send me a text.
4. They studied the English irregular verbs ___________ they knew them well.
5. ___________ you exercise regularly, you will stay fit.
6. Ravi took great care of his mother, ___________ he was only eight.

Take Note
The conjunction **although** says something surprising about an activity or happening, e.g. We enjoyed the film **although** it was scary.

B. Complete each sentence with a suitable group of words to match the **conjunction**.

shall I come to yours	I brush your hair	she meets you tonight
Dad stayed indoors	I got up late	he was too tired
the doctor says you may	you seem to have lost some weight	

1. I missed my bus because ______________________________.
2. Jim tried to go on working but ______________________________.
3. Stand still while ______________________________.
4. Would you like to come to my house or ______________________________?
5. Ria will tell you all about the party when

______________________________.

6. You're looking well, though

______________________________.

7. Please don't attend school until

______________________________.

8. It was snowing, so

______________________________.

Think & Share Get into pairs and write down some common conjunctions on slips of paper. Place these face down on the table. Ask your partner to make a sentence and say it aloud. Then turn over one of the slips and make a sentence to match your partner's sentence, using the conjunction given on the slip. Swap roles with your partner and continue the game.

  ISBN 978-93-5103-602-9

9 Sentences

Let's Recall

- A **sentence** is divided into **subject** and **predicate**.
- The **subject** is the noun, pronoun or group of words that the sentence is about. The **predicate** is the part of the sentence that contains the verb. It tells us something about the subject.
- A verb must agree with its subject. A singular subject has a singular verb and a plural subject has a plural verb.

9.1 Revising sentences

1. Underline the **subject** and double-underline the **predicate** in each sentence.

   a. The headmistress of the school will speak to each one of you.
   b. People with pets should keep them under control.
   c. I forgot to bring my gym kit with me today.
   d. Alisha and her mum looked everywhere for her ballet shoes.
   e. Javed and Junaid are twins.
   f. Fishing takes a lot of patience.
   g. The snow is turning the landscape completely white.
   h. In through the window flew a bird.

Take Note

- The predicate can come before the subject, e.g. **Round the corner came** a taxi.
- The subject can be a long word group, e.g. **The people living on this planet** must try to prevent climate change.

2. Complete each sentence with a suitable **subject**.

   a. ____________________ is the capital of Australia.
   b. ____________________ is my favourite TV show.
   c. ____________________ is called a duckling.
   d. ____________________ live in Dubai.
   e. ____________________ is the highest mountain in the world.
   f. ____________________ live in a stable.

3. Underline the **subject** and circle the **verb** it agrees with in each sentence.

   a. Dad takes us to school every day.
   b. He likes to sketch the people at the metro station.

ISBN 978-93-5103-602-9

c. News spreads fast in this small town.
d. My sister and I jog in this park every morning.
e. Most people agree that watching television all day is bad for you.
f. Five thousand rupees is too high a price for an old cupboard like that.
g. These trousers are too tight for me now.
h. The furniture for our new house has been delivered.

4. Circle the correct **verb** to complete each sentence.
a. (Were / Was) you caught in the traffic?
b. Many Disney characters (participates / participate) in the parade at Disneyland.
c. All squares (have / has) four equal sides.
d. Both the helper and my baby sister (has / have) fallen asleep.
e. Sand, water and cement (is / are) mixed to make concrete.
f. Air pollution (is / are) becoming a major health hazard in the city.

5. Fill in the blanks with the correct form of the **verbs** given in the box below. You may use some verbs more than once.

perform	are	buy	is	chat
jostle	cheer	go		

Yesterday evening, my brother and I ___________ to a live performance by a rock band. There ___________ a long line for the tickets. Two hours ___________ a long time to stand in line, so we ___________ with some of the people around us. My brother ___________ a pack of fruit juice from a shop close by. Inside, the auditorium ___________ buzzing with voices as people ___________ for seats. Soon the curtains ___________ up and everyone ___________. The band ___________ introduced to the audience by the manager of the auditorium. It ___________ some of its greatest hits. The audience ___________ delighted.

Take Note
- Group nouns like orchestra and audience can have a plural verb, e.g. The orchestra **are** tuning up. The audience **were** laughing loudly.
- Amounts usually have a singular verb, e.g. Twenty rupees **is** enough for the bus fare.

 ISBN 978-93-5103-602-9

9.2 Phrases

Read the story.

Tom and **his brother Jack** were climbing **a steep hill**. Jack was **quite exhausted**.

At the top of the hill they rested **on the platform**. Tom divided his banana **between them**.

Before leaving, Jack put **the banana skin** carefully **into the dustbin**.

What could happen if Jack did not put the banana skin into the dustbin?

Who was climbing with Tom?

Where did they rest?

Where did Jack put the banana skin?

1. Tick the groups of words that do NOT make complete sense.

   a. Jack was quite exhausted ☐

   b. At the top of the hill ☐

   c. Tom divided his banana between them ☐

   d. On the platform ☐

   e. Into the dustbin ☐

Remember!

A group of words that makes complete sense is called a **sentence**. A sentence starts with a capital letter and usually ends with a full stop.

2. Choose a suitable group of words from the box below to complete each sentence.

a map of Delhi	drinking milk	after the fight
my bunch of keys	my sister	

   a. I've lost ______________________________.

   b. ______________________________ is arriving tomorrow.

   c. The tourist asked Dorji where he could buy ______________________.

   d. ______________________________ is good for your health.

   e. ______________________________ Vijay came home with a torn shirt.

A group of words that has meaning but does not make complete sense is called a **phrase**.

 ISBN 978-93-5103-602-9

Let's Practise

A. Look at each group of words. In the brackets, write **S** if it is a sentence or **P** if it is a phrase.

> **Take Note**
> A phrase does not have a subject or predicate.

1. The shop assistant handed me a bag [ ]
2. Would like [ ]
3. My new laptop is easy to use [ ]
4. We put our food waste into special recycling bins [ ]
5. A bag of potatoes [ ]
6. Take all your luggage with you [ ]
7. A pink T-shirt [ ]
8. From the kitchen [ ]
9. A banana divided in half [ ]
10. I will go [ ]

B. Complete each sentence with a **phrase** from the box below.

the principal	from cover to cover	a green suit
in my garden	quite amusing	Dad's desk
your luggage	members of the drama society	
my favourite team	a swarm	

1. ____________________ I grow fruit and vegetables.
2. I read the book ____________________.
3. Several of my friends are ____________________.
4. I found the story ____________________.
5. Do you see that man in ____________________?
6. ____________________ won the basketball match.
7. A group of bees is called ____________________.
8. ____________________ called me into his office this morning.
9. Take all ____________________ with you.
10. I left the letter on ____________________.

Think & Share Pair up with a classmate. You each write down a sentence on a sheet of paper, underline a phrase in it and then hand it over to your partner. Then you each make a new sentence with the marked-out phrase and repeat the game.

 ISBN 978-93-5103-602-9

9.3 Types of sentences

Read the story.

How do you think Ginny feels now?

What did Jill ask?
What did Ginny reply?
What did Jill say when she found Ginny's contact lens?

1. From the story above, find the following.
   a. A sentence that states a fact: ______________________
   b. A sentence that has the word "not": ______________________
   c. A sentence that asks a question: ______________________
   d. A sentence that gives an order: ______________________
   e. A sentence that expresses excitement: ______________________

2. Match the following.

a.	The Statue of Liberty •	• i.	the *Mona Lisa*?
b.	Mahatma Gandhi never •	• ii.	a magnificent sight!
c.	Have you seen •	• iii.	is in New York.
d.	Bring me •	• iv.	told a lie.
e.	What •	• v.	that book at once.

A sentence that makes a statement is an **assertive** or **declarative sentence**. A sentence that makes a negative statement, using **not** or **never**, is a **negative sentence**. A sentence that asks a question is an **interrogative sentence**. A sentence that expresses a strong feeling and ends with an exclamation mark is an **exclamatory sentence**. A sentence that gives an order or command is an **imperative sentence**.

 ISBN 978-93-5103-602-9

Let's Practise

A. In the brackets, write **A** for assertive, **N** for negative, **I** for interrogative, **E** for exclamatory or **Im** for imperative.

1. What a sweet child! [ ]
2. Oysters are not my favourite food. [ ]
3. Which book did you get from the library? [ ]
4. The weather is going to improve soon. [ ]
5. Finish your homework. [ ]
6. Where is the Bermuda Triangle? [ ]
7. Mandy cannot run fast. [ ]
8. How pretty this dress is! [ ]

Take Note

- In imperative sentences, the subject **you** is not usually mentioned, e.g. Open the door.
- In exclamatory sentences, the verb is sometimes not mentioned, e.g. What a nuisance!

B. Answer each interrogative sentence with an **assertive sentence**. Begin your answer with **Yes**.

Example Have you tidied your bedroom?

Yes, I have tidied my bedroom.

1. Are you learning English at school?

 ____

2. Did you see that film?

 ____

3. Have you finished your project?

 ____

4. Was the phone ringing?

 ____

5. Should we go and visit Grandmother?

 ____

6. Is your father at home today?

 ____

7. Were her clothes dirty?

 ____

8. Can you see the lighthouse?

 ____

 ISBN 978-93-5103-602-9

C. Change each assertive sentence into an **exclamatory sentence**.

Example John is a clever boy.

What a clever boy John is!

1. They were brave explorers.

____

2. She makes a lovely bride.

____

3. I have been foolish.

____

4. Harry was a lazy child.

____

5. That was an exceptional film.

____

6. Julie is a beautiful baby.

____

Take Note
Exclamatory sentences usually start with a **wh-word**, such as what or how. In such sentences, the word order changes round, e.g. How pale the sky looks!

D. Change each assertive sentence into a **negative sentence**.

Example The sun has gone down.

The sun has not gone down.

1. It is very warm today.

____

2. We have visited Disneyland before.

____

3. They agree with me on this matter.

____

4. Sohrab was listening to the lecture attentively.

____

5. My music teacher changed the time of my lesson.

____

6. Dev likes getting up early.

____

Take Note
If there is a helping verb in the sentence, we put **not** after it, e.g. He **is not** going to the gym. If there is no helping verb, we use **do, does** or **did** as the helping verb, e.g. I **do not** like oysters.

10 Questions

Let's Recall

- An interrogative sentence is also called a **question**.
- When we form a question, we usually change the order of the words and place the verb first.

10.1 Revising questions

1. Form a **question** by changing the order of the words in each sentence.

Take Note
If the question has a helping verb, we put the subject between the helping verb and the main verb, e.g. **Is** Roshan **going** to the party?

Example Misha is a good chess player.

Is Misha a good chess player?

a. Vasu is planning to study in Australia.

____

b. There are plenty of good restaurants in this town.

____

c. It was a great film.

____

d. There were lots of people at the show yesterday.

____

e. I am taller than Jean.

____

f. There is a baby-changing room here.

____

g. It was Mrs Kaul's first car.

____

h. There were many film stars at the opening ceremony.

____

i. I am invited to Sohail's party too.

____

j. Jim was snoring last night.

____

 ISBN 978-93-5103-602-9

10.2 Questions (1)

Read the story.

Alice was shopping for a present for her sister. "**Do** you have any books on horses?" she asked.

"Here you are," said the salesman. "Thanks. **Do** you have any books on tennis?" asked Alice.

"**Does** this book cover Wimbledon?" asked Alice. "Yes, it does," said the salesman.

What does Alice's sister like? How do you know?

What did Alice first ask the salesman?

What else did Alice want to know?

What did Alice ask about the book on tennis?

1. Rewrite each sentence as a question. Use the correct form of the verb **do**.

   Example Alice wanted a book for her sister.

   Did Alice want a book for her sister?

   a. The shop stocked books about tennis and horses.

   ____

   b. Alice chose two books.

   ____

   c. The salesman showed Alice the books in the sports section.

   ____

2. Read the question. Underline the main verb.

   a. Did you see the aeroplane?

   b. Does your dad know about your new friend?

   c. Do the children want a ride on the roller coaster?

Questions formed with the helping verbs **do/does/did** use the basic form of the main verb. The answer often repeats the words used in the question, for example, "Did you find your watch?" "Yes, I found my watch."

 ISBN 978-93-5103-602-9

Let's Practise

A. Answer each **question**. Begin with **Yes** or **No** as indicated in the brackets.

Example Did you see the eclipse of the sun? (Yes)

Yes, I saw the eclipse of the sun.

1. Does your mum play the piano? (No)

____

2. Do you often see your grandmother? (Yes)

____

3. Did the thunder frighten you? (No)

____

4. Do you like that dog? (Yes)

____

Take Note

- In questions formed with **do/does/did**, the subject follows the helping verb.
- Such questions are often answered with a simple **Yes** or **No**.

B. Form a **question** for each sentence. Use the helping verb **do**, **does** or **did**.

Example Do you go skating every evening?

Yes, I go skating every evening.

1. _______________

Yes, the postman delivered the letter this morning.

2. _______________

No, Tom did not do well in the exam.

3. _______________

Yes, he visits his grandfather every Sunday.

4. _______________

No, it did not rain yesterday.

5. _______________

Yes, I play football every day.

6. _______________

No, she did not finish her work.

C. Fill in each blank with **do**, **does** or **did**.

1. ________ the children go to the park yesterday?
2. ________ you know where the post office is?
3. ________ the library close early on a Tuesday?
4. ________ it often snow in Kashmir?

 ISBN 978-93-5103-602-9

10.3 Questions (2)

Remember!
The **-ing** form of a verb is called the present participle. The past participle of a regular verb ends with **-ed**. The simple past and past participle of irregular verbs may be the same or different from each other.

Read the story.

"**Have** you **kept** us a table for two?" asked Ken. "Yes, we have," said the waiter.

"**Has** it **been** a busy day today?" asked Ken. "Yes, it has," said the waiter.

"**Have** you **tried** seafood here before?" asked Ken. "No, I haven't, but I want to," said Laura.

Do you think Laura liked the seafood?

What did Ken ask the waiter first?

Why do you think it was a busy day at the restaurant?

What did Ken ask Laura?

1. Complete each question with the help of the answer given.
   a. No, I'm afraid we haven't got a table by the window.
   Have you ____
   ____
   b. Yes, the menu has changed since you last visited the restaurant.
   Has ____
   ____
   c. Yes, the lobsters had been taken off the menu when you last came.
   Had the ____
   ____

2. Fill in each blank with a helping verb. Underline the main verb.
   a. ______________ Peter shown you his drawing?
   b. ______________ they received full instructions before they began the work?
   c. ______________ you cleaned the flat already?

Questions formed with the helping verbs **have/has/had** use the past participle of the main verb. They are used to refer to a happening in the past.

 ISBN 978-93-5103-602-9

Let's Practise

A. Form a **question** for each sentence. Use the helping verb **has**, **have** or **had**.

> **Take Note**
> In questions formed with **have/has/had**, the subject follows the helping verb.

Example I have finished my breakfast.

Have you finished your breakfast?

1. I have seen the latest issue of the school magazine.

    ____

2. Shelly has invited Kartik to her party this Saturday.

    ____

3. Amit has done his homework.

    ____

4. The girls have cleaned their room this morning.

    ____

5. The principal had met the new pupils before the beginning of term.

    ____

B. Complete each **question** with a helping verb from the box. You may use some helping verbs more than once. Circle the main verb.

has	have	had

1. __________ you checked the time on your watch?
2. __________ you asked your mum for permission?
3. __________ Sheila finished washing the clothes?
4. __________ they paid their bills yet?
5. __________ we stayed in this hotel before?
6. __________ someone been using my computer?
7. __________ he completed his project before he went on leave?
8. __________ they already discussed the problem before yesterday's meeting?

Think & Share Make three flash cards with the helping verbs **have**, **has** or **had** written on them and keep them face down on a table. Pair up with a classmate and hand each other a slip of paper with a noun (subject) and a suitable action word (main verb) written on it. Then pick up a flash card and make a question with the helping verb written on it and the words written on the slip of paper.

 ISBN 978-93-5103-602-9

11 Punctuation

Let's Recall

- We use an **exclamation mark (!)** after greetings and expressions of strong feeling.
- We use an **apostrophe** (') with **-s** to show possession.
- We also use an apostrophe to join two words to make a short form. The apostrophe is used for the missing letters.
- We use **commas** (,) in lists of things.

11.1 Revising punctuation

1. Add a **full stop** or an **exclamation mark** wherever necessary.

   a. I don't think I will be able to go to work today

   b. How green the grass is

   c. There's a car blocking the driveway

   d. What a relief

   e. Happy birthday

2. Fill in each blank with the correct **possessive** form.

   a. the apron belonging to the waitress: the ____________ apron

   b. clothes for children: ____________ clothes

   c. uniforms for soldiers: ____________ uniforms

   d. the laptop belonging to Cyrus: ____________ laptop

   e. the cars belonging to the people: the ____________ cars

   f. the bags belonging to the Singhs: the ____________ bags

   g. magazines for women: ____________ magazines

   h. the crown belonging to the princess: the ____________ crown

Remember!

- With plural nouns ending in **-s**, we add only the apostrophe ('), e.g. the Browns' flat.
- With plural nouns not ending in **-s**, we add **'s**, e.g. people**'s** opinions.
- With singular nouns ending in **-s**, we add **'s**, e.g. my boss's door.

3. Match the **short form** with its full form.

a. she'll •	•	i. they will
b. we'll •	•	ii. you will
c. I'll •	•	iii. we shall/will
d. you'll •	•	iv. she will
e. they'll •	•	v. I shall/will

 ISBN 978-93-5103-602-9

11.2 More about short forms

Read the story.

Harry **couldn't** find his blue ruler. He was upset as he **didn't** have a spare one.

Harry **couldn't** go to school without a ruler. "I **don't** have a blue ruler, but here is a red one," said the saleslady.

The next day, Harry found his old ruler. "I **shouldn't** have bought a new ruler!" he said.

How do you think Harry felt when he found his old ruler?

Why was Harry upset?

Why did the saleslady give him a red ruler?

What did he say when he found the blue ruler?

1. Note the highlighted short forms in the story above. Now circle the correct short form to complete each sentence.
   a. Harry (couldn't / could'nt) go to school without his ruler.
   b. Harry (didn't / did'nt) search properly for his ruler.
   c. The saleslady (had'nt / hadn't) got a blue ruler.
   d. Harry (shouldn't / should'nt) have bought a new ruler.
   e. (I amn't / I'm not) going to the gym today.

2. Circle the short form in each sentence. Then write the full form in the blank.
   a. He won't be able to arrive in time. ________________
   b. You needn't worry about him so much. ________________
   c. The police can't catch the thief. ________________
   d. We shan't have lunch right now. ________________
   e. He wouldn't allow me to speak. ________________

Take Note

- **Can not** is usually written as one word, **cannot** or **can't**.
- **Will not** becomes **won't**, and **shall not** becomes **shan't**.
- **I am not** becomes **I'm not**.

In negative sentences, the verbs are usually shortened by adding **not** to the helping verb and then replacing the **o** in **not** with an apostrophe, for example, **should** + **not** = **shouldn't**.

ISBN 978-93-5103-602-9

Let's Practise

A. Complete the table.

	Full form	Short form		Full form	Short form
1.	cannot		6.		shan't
2.		couldn't	7.	should not	
3.	did not		8.	was not	
4.		mustn't	9.	will not	
5.	need not		10.		wouldn't

B. Fill in each blank with a **short form**. Use the verb form given in the brackets.

1. ________ Sumeet need new shoes? (does not)
2. Dad ________ find his car. (could not)
3. I ________ be coming to the meeting this afternoon. (shall not)
4. It ________ take long to do this exercise. (will not)
5. You ________ tell anyone. (must not)
6. ________ the plant growing well? (is not)
7. I ________ understand the message. (cannot)
8. People ________ leave litter in public places. (should not)

C. Fill in each blank with a suitable negative **short form**. The answer to the question will help you.

Example Don't you want to see the film?
Yes, I do.

1. ________ you finished that letter yet?
   Yes, I have.
2. ________ they insured the car?
   Yes, they had.
3. ________ Chitra be going to Nadia's party?
   Yes, she will.
4. ________ the washing machine finished yet?
   Yes, it has.
5. ________ you staying at home tonight?
   Yes, I am.

Take Note
We can use negative short forms in questions, e.g. **Don't** you want to come with me? Questions like this expect the answer **yes**.

 ISBN 978-93-5103-602-9

11.3 The comma

Read the story.

Liz, **Sally's new neighbour,** has just moved from Newtown. She has joined Sally's school.

"**Liz,** do you like English?" Sally asked. "**Yes,** I do," said Liz.

Mr Thomas, **the English teacher,** took the first class. "Pay attention, **please**," he said.

Remember!
Commas mark the pauses we make when we are speaking. We also use commas in a list, e.g. scissors, glue, paper, pencils and rulers.

Do you think Sally is a good friend?

Who has just moved from Newtown?

What did Sally say to Liz?

Who took the first class? What did he tell the children?

1. Look at the commas in the story again. Now add a comma wherever necessary in each sentence.
   a. Sally and Liz the new friends sit together in class.
   b. "Liz have you seen our gym?" asks Sally.
   c. "No I haven't. Will you show me please?" replies Liz.

2. Add a comma wherever necessary.
   a. Please close the door Peter.
   b. The house that has a garden in front belongs to Maya.
   c. Yes I have received your letter.
   d. Now listen to me carefully.
   e. Hello Tom where are you going?
   f. No I have not met Alisha yet.
   g. Thank you Helen very much.
   h. James the boy with the curly hair is my friend.

We use **commas** before and after a group of words that describes a person, or when addressing somebody by their name. A comma also separates brief expressions, such as **yes, no, please** and **thank you**.

 ISBN 978-93-5103-602-9

Let's Practise

A. Rewrite each sentence using **commas** wherever necessary.

1. Harry Potter the boy wizard is a popular storybook character.
2. Beena my best friend is coming to visit me next week.
3. Yes Eddie you have passed the exam. Well done!
4. No you may not play football Rahul.
5. No I don't need any lunch thank you.
6. Take a seat please Mr Das.

B. Rewrite each sentence using **commas** and other punctuation in the right place.

1. yes I will go to the market today
2. hi reema did you have a good holiday
3. miss gupta our gym teacher wouldn't let us climb the ropes
4. we are making cards for our parents teachers and friends
5. thank you mr khan for all your suggestions
6. dr varma our doctor has come to see grandmother

Think & Share Pair up with a classmate. Make up five sentences whose meaning changes just by adding a comma.

Example Let's eat Grandmother.
Let's eat, Grandmother.

 ISBN 978-93-5103-602-9

Review 3

1. Fill in each blank with a **preposition** from the box below.

beside	up	with	besides	down	to
at	around	from	behind		

a. Take that knife away ____________ the baby!

b. ____________ my piano lessons, I'm learning to play the flute.

c. The children's toys were lying all ____________ the room.

d. Put the breakfast tray on the table ____________ Grandfather's bed.

e. We stopped for a rest halfway ____________ the hill.

f. I was ____________ Meena in the queue.

g. The meeting ____________ the town hall was cancelled.

h. We walked ____________ the steps till we reached the ground floor.

i. Please give this note ____________ your mother.

j. Akshay is dancing ____________ Uma.

2. Look at each underlined word. Tick the correct box to indicate if it is a **preposition** or an **adverb**.

	Preposition	Adverb
a. Tears ran <u>down</u> the little girl's cheeks.	☐	☐
b. "You're most welcome to come in and look <u>around</u>," said the sculptor.	☐	☐
c. What goes up must come <u>down</u>.	☐	☐
d. My grandmother's waiting <u>outside</u> the gate to pick me up.	☐	☐
e. They walked <u>around</u> the garden, admiring the flowers.	☐	☐
f. I went <u>outside</u> to get some fresh air.	☐	☐

 ISBN 978-93-5103-602-9

3. Tick the correct **conjunction** to complete each sentence.

a. Send me a postcard _____ you go to London.

i. at　　ii. although　　iii. when

b. _____ we were on holiday, we did a lot of swimming.

i. Until　　ii. If　　iii. While

c. Joe kept on working _____ it was time to go home.

i. until　　ii. as　　iii. while

d. We can come tomorrow _____ you are not at home today.

i. while　　ii. because　　iii. if

e. Tom decided to finish his assignment _____ it was very late.

i. as　　ii. although　　iii. while

4. Join each pair of sentences with the **conjunction** given in the brackets.

a. I learnt French. I was at school. (when)

____

b. The fields will flood. It goes on raining. (if)

____

c. She went on working. She was tired. (although)

____

d. I can't set the table. Clear away your books. (until)

____

e. You can peel the potatoes. You're watching television. (while)

____

5. Complete each sentence with a group of words from the box below.

it is difficult	I looked in the mirror	you come back
she was intelligent	I do my homework	
Vikas does well in his exams	we hurry	it was too late

a. When __________________, I saw spots all over my face.

b. I sometimes have the radio on while __________________.

c. I didn't phone Mita because __________________.

d. I enjoy Maths, although __________________.

ISBN 978-93-5103-602-9

e. I'll wait here until ______________.

f. We'll catch the earlier train if ______________.

g. Although ______________, Diana didn't want to go to university.

h. If ______________, he plans to go backpacking across India in the summer break!

6. Write a sentence for each **phrase** below.

a. letter from my best friend

____

b. scattered all over the floor

____

c. in less than a month

____

d. for his final exams

____

e. lying across the road

____

f. slowed down to make way for the ambulance

____

7. Read each sentence. In the brackets, write **A** for assertive, **N** for negative, **I** for interrogative, **E** for exclamatory or **Im** for imperative.

a. Are you ready to go out with me? [ ]

b. I've just won the lottery! [ ]

c. Not every story gets printed. [ ]

d. Give this book back to the teacher. [ ]

e. We had salad and roast potatoes for lunch. [ ]

f. What a wonderful film it was! [ ]

g. Did you know that butterflies taste with their feet? [ ]

h. I have never seen such a frisky dog. [ ]

8. Choose a **helping verb** from the box below to begin each **question**.

did	does	have	has	do	had

a. __________ you want me to help you?

b. __________ you brushed your teeth?

c. __________ they visit the Taj Mahal yesterday?

 ISBN 978-93-5103-602-9

d. ____________ the Earth move around the sun?

e. ____________ the car been cleaned today?

f. ____________ they finished dinner by the time you arrived?

9. Rewrite each sentence as a **question**. Begin with a suitable **helping verb**.

Example Mum has taken her suit to the cleaner's.

Has Mum taken her suit to the cleaner's?

a. Harry did his homework last night.

____

b. They had seen this film earlier.

____

c. The shop opens late at weekends.

____

d. The children travel to school by bus.

____

e. We have got enough water for the journey.

____

10. Add **commas** and **apostrophes** wherever necessary.

a. Paris the capital of France is a beautiful city.

b. Peters mum works at the bank.

c. David Beckham the famous footballer coached the junior team.

d. Whos taken my boots? Theyre not in the cupboard.

e. The girls instructor was teaching them to swim.

f. Theres been no rain for a week.

Spot the Error

11. There is a mistake in each sentence. Underline it and rewrite the passage correctly in your notebook.

Last week I went beside my class to visit the museum. We wanted to learn about rocks so we were doing a project in Geography. Mr Rao the museum director welcomed us. He led us down the stairs to the top floor and showed us a video about the movement of the continents. Does you know that many years ago the continents were grouped tightly together? Over millions of years they slowly break away from each other. It was fascinating but we all enjoyed the video. It just shows that you should consider every theory seriously?

 ISBN 978-93-5103-602-9

12 Comprehension

12.1 Identifying the main idea and sequencing

- There are many ideas in a text, but you should try to find the one idea that links them. This is called identifying the main idea.
- To understand fully what you read, you must be able to work out the order in which events happen. This is called sequencing.

Take Note

A poster
- uses language that is direct and catchy.
- uses bullet points and subheadings to organise the information.
- uses pictures to attract the reader's attention.

Read the poster.

CROSSING THE ROAD

Do you know how to cross the road?
- Find a zebra crossing.
- Wait for the traffic light to indicate that it is safe to cross.
- Step on to the road only when all vehicles have stopped.
- Walk across briskly. **DO NOT** run!

What if there is no zebra crossing?
- Wait at the kerb.
- Look right, look left, look right again.
- When you are sure there are no vehicles coming, **walk** across.

Do you want to learn?
Come over for a fun workshop on traffic safety.
When: 10–11 a.m., 25 October 2016
Where: Sector 19 Police Station, Chandigarh

 ISBN 978-93-5103-602-9

Answer the questions.

1. What is the main idea of the poster? Tick the correct answer.
   a. How to read a traffic signal
   b. How to use a zebra crossing
   c. How to cross a road

2. What is the main idea of the first subheading?

   ____

   ____

Think!
In order to identify the main idea, you
- read the text. Then ask yourself, "What is it mainly about?"
- look at the title. A good title often tells you what the text is about.

3. What should you do if there is no zebra crossing?

   ____

   ____

4. How can you learn more about traffic safety?

   ____

   ____

5. In the brackets, number the sentences in the correct order.
   a. Look left. [ ]
   b. When there are no vehicles coming, walk across. [ ]
   c. Look right. [ ]
   d. Look right again. [ ]

Think!
In order to work out the sequence of events, you
- make sure you understand which events you need to sequence.
- work out how these events are related.
- look for numbering or the order in which the events are placed.

6. What does the word **kerb** mean? Tick the correct answer.
   a. crossing
   b. edge of a pavement
   c. road

7. Identify the type of sentence. Tick the correct answer.
   a. Wait at the kerb.
      i. assertive ii. interrogative iii. imperative
   b. When you are sure there are no vehicles coming, walk across.
      i. assertive ii. interrogative iii. imperative
   c. Do you want to learn?
      i. assertive ii. interrogative iii. imperative

8. Find and write down two compound nouns from the poster.

   ____________________ ____________________

 ISBN 978-93-5103-602-9

12.2 Predicting and finding similarities and differences

- As you read a story, it is important to understand what is happening in it and try to think what might happen next. This is called predicting.
- To help you understand what you read, you need to compare things and think about how they are alike or different. This is called finding similarities and differences.

Read the review.

Book: *The Best of Tagore*
Author: Jharna Basu
Publisher: Scholastic

"Kabuliwala" is the opening story in this collection of Tagore's short stories. Translated by Jharna Basu from the original in Bengali, this timeless tale is the perfect introduction for young readers to the magical world of Rabindranath Tagore.

Set in Calcutta in the 1900s, "Kabuliwala" is about the loving bond between a little girl and a big burly Afghan. Rahmat, known to everyone as the Kabuliwala, leaves his beloved daughter and comes to India with his wares to earn the money he needs to support his family in Afghanistan. He meets a little girl named Mini, who reminds him of his own daughter back home. Mini is afraid of him at first, but she is also curious, and soon the two become close friends. One day Rahmat gets caught up in a brawl and is put in jail. On his release a few years later, he comes to see Mini, but discovers that she has grown up and is to be married that day. She is now very different from the lively little child he used to know. He realises that his own daughter must have grown up too. Mini's father understands his feelings and gives him money to go home to his daughter.

Take Note

A review
- gives information about the subject.
- gives the writer's opinion on the subject.
- may be written in the first person.
- aims at persuading or convincing the reader.

 ISBN 978-93-5103-602-9

The story was made into a Hindi film with the same title in 1961. The film follows the original story closely, but is built up with details of the Kabuliwala's life in Afghanistan. In the film, he is forced to sell off his property to pay for the treatment of his daughter Ameena. He comes to Calcutta to peddle his wares. While Tagore's story shows Mini's mother treating the Kabuliwala with mistrust and suspicion, the film highlights this further by including a dramatic scene where Mini's family thinks he has kidnapped her.

Written more than a century ago, "Kabuliwala" is a simple and moving story that touches our hearts even today.

Answer the questions.

1. Do you think Mini and Rahmat would have continued their friendship if Rahmat had not been sent to jail? Support your answer with a detail from the story.

   ____

   ____

2. Do you think Rahmat's daughter will recognise him when he goes back to his home in Afghanistan? Give one reason for your answer.

   ____

   ____

3. List one way in which the book and the film are similar and different.

   Similarity: ______________________________

   Difference: ______________________________

4. What does the word **brawl** mean? Tick the correct answer.

   a. a rough fight b. a quarrel c. a chase

5. List the adjectives that are used to describe

   a. the Kabuliwala: ______________________________

   ____

   b. Mini: ______________________________

   ____

6. Find four abstract nouns in the story and make sentences with them.

   a. ______________________________

   b. ______________________________

   c. ______________________________

   d. ______________________________

Think!
In order to predict, you
- find information related to the question.
- think about the information and ask yourself, "What is the writer suggesting might happen?"

Think!
In order to find similarities and differences, you
- make notes on what you know about the things you are comparing.
- compare your points for each.
- decide how alike or different the things are.

 ISBN 978-93-5103-602-9

12.3 Concluding and summarising

- As you read a text, you should think carefully about the facts and details and decide what they actually mean. This is called concluding.
- When you talk about what you have read, you need to put together the main points in as few words as possible. This is called summarising.

Read the article.

How the Teddy Bear Got Its Name

Teddy bears are among the best loved of children's toys, given as presents the world over. Behind this cute and cuddly toy lies an interesting story. One day in 1902, President Theodore Roosevelt (nicknamed "Teddy") of the United States went on a hunting trip with a friend. The guide caught a bear and asked the president to shoot it, but he refused because he felt it would be unsportsmanlike.

The story of his kind act became famous and a cartoon of the incident appeared in *The Washington Post*. A Brooklyn shopkeeper made a bear cub from furry material and put it in the shop window with the label "Teddy's Bear". Someone bought it immediately, and soon everybody wanted one. The shopkeeper made more, and got the president's permission to call them "teddy bears".

The following year, a toy manufacturer in Germany, who had already been making toy bears, exhibited them at a toy fair in Leipzig, Germany. An American in the toy business saw them and had many of them imported to the United States. So that was how teddy bears became a favourite toy all over the world.

Take Note

An article

- presents detailed information and ideas about a topic.
- uses simple, clear language, as if it is talking directly to the reader.
- is usually about a famous personality or a matter of general interest.

 ISBN 978-93-5103-602-9

Answer the questions.

1. You can conclude that the reason why everybody suddenly wanted a bear like the one in the shop window was
   a. the bear in the window was furry and cuddly.
   b. the bear in the window looked like the bear in the cartoon in *The Washington Post*.
   c. the shopkeeper used the label "Teddy's Bear" to link his bear with the story of President Roosevelt's hunting trip.

Think!
In order to conclude, you
- understand what you are making a conclusion about.
- find the facts and details from the text.
- decide what exactly the facts and details mean.

2. How can you conclude that President Roosevelt was a kind-hearted man?

____

____

____

3. How can you conclude that the toy bear was named after President Roosevelt?

____

____

____

Think!
In order to summarise, you
- look carefully at the information in the text.
- decide on what is important and how it is connected.
- leave out any unnecessary information.

4. Write a short summary of the story of how teddy bears got their name.

____

____

____

____

____

____

____

____

5. Which sentence would you leave out of a summary of the first paragraph? Tick the correct answer.
   a. Theodore Roosevelt was the president of the United States.
   b. Theodore Roosevelt went on a hunting trip.
   c. The hunting party's guide caught a bear.
   d. Theodore Roosevelt refused to shoot the bear.

 ISBN 978-93-5103-602-9

6. Which sentence would you NOT use in a summary of the second paragraph? Tick the correct answer.

   a. The story about the hunting trip became famous.

   b. A Brooklyn shopkeeper made toy bears.

   c. The shopkeeper named his toy bear "Teddy's Bear".

   d. An American businessman imported toy bears from Germany to the United States.

7. What does the word **unsportsmanlike** mean? Tick the correct answer.

   a. unkind b. poor in sports c. unfair

8. Find the possessive forms of three nouns in the article and write them in the blanks.

   a. ____________ b. ____________ c. ____________

9. Find a concrete uncountable noun and an abstract uncountable noun in the second paragraph, and write them in the blanks.

   a. ____________________ b. ____________________

10. Find three prepositions of place in the article and make sentences with them.

   a. ____

   b. ____

   c. ____

11. Fill in the missing verb forms.

	Simple past (singular and plural)	Past continuous (singular)	Past perfect (singular and plural)
a.	became		
b.	bought		
c.	caught		
d.	felt		
e.	gave		
f.	got		
g.	made		
h.	put		
i.	saw		
j.	went		

 ISBN 978-93-5103-602-9

12.4 Finding information and distinguishing between fact and opinion

- When you are asked about a certain thing in the text, you read it again and find the correct details. This is called finding information.
- When you read, you should try to understand the difference between what is true and what someone believes is true. This is called distinguishing between fact and opinion.

Take Note

A newspaper report
- has a headline that gives the reader an idea of the story.
- is short and presented in an easy-to-read style.
- describes past events that really happened.
- uses facts and figures to support the given information.

Read the newspaper report.

Daylight Robbery at City Bank

CAUGHT RED-HANDED: The two robbers were arrested by the police.

New Delhi: Customers and staff at City Bank on MG Road were doing business as usual yesterday at 2.15 p.m., when two men wearing masks and armed with guns burst in. They headed straight to the cashier and ordered her to hand over ten lakh rupees.

Melanie D'Costa, the threatened cashier, told them to wait as that amount of money was not available at the counter and she would have to order it. The brave cashier kept the intruders talking at the counter while another employee secretly telephoned the police. The police were already entering MG Road when somebody activated the bank's alarm system. Terrified by the noise, the two men tried to run out of the bank. However, they ran straight into the arms of the police, who had by then surrounded the bank. The police arrested them immediately and took them to the police station.

Later, when congratulated on her courage, Melanie, 23, said she was not particularly brave. She had acted as any other person would. "It was just common sense," she added. The bank manager told this reporter that Melanie would be receiving an award for her bravery at a special function next week.

 ISBN 978-93-5103-602-9

Answer the questions.

1. How did Melanie avoid handing over the money to the robbers? Tick the correct answer.
   a. She hid the cash.
   b. She asked a colleague to call the police.
   c. She kept the intruders talking.
   d. She raised the alarm.

2. How did the police get to know about the robbery?

   ____

   ____

3. How did the robbers get caught by the police?

   ____

   ____

4. Read each statement. In the brackets, write **F** if it is a fact or **O** if it is an opinion.
   a. The two masked men carried guns. [ ]
   b. The cashier was a brave woman. [ ]
   c. The police arrested the two masked men. [ ]
   d. The cashier had acted as any other person would. [ ]
   e. Melanie was 23 years old. [ ]

5. How would you describe Melanie's character? Mention a fact to support your opinion.

   ____

   ____

6. What does Melanie mean when she says she used her **common sense**?

   ____

   ____

7. Identify the tense of each sentence and write it in the blank.
   a. The police had surrounded the bank. ____________
   b. Melanie will be receiving an award next week. ____________

8. Circle the subject and underline the predicate.
   a. Melanie D'Costa, the threatened cashier, told them to wait.
   b. Terrified by the noise, the two men ran out of the front door of the bank.

Think!

In order to find information, you

- underline the keywords in the question. They will tell you what information you need to find.
- find those keywords in the text.
- carefully read the information given in the sentence and decide on the answer.

Think!

In order to distinguish between fact and opinion, you

- check if the statement can be proved to be true. If it can be proved, it is a fact.
- check if the statement expresses what someone thinks or believes. If it cannot be proved to be correct, it is an opinion.

 ISBN 978-93-5103-602-9

13 Composition

13.1 Report

A report is a description of something that you have observed, heard, done or studied.

Take Note
A typical report has three main parts:
1. Introduction
2. Body
3. Conclusion

Bonsai Plants

Bonsai is the art of growing a small-sized tree in a pot or container. The word "bonsai" comes from a Japanese expression that means "planting in a tray".

Introduction
Present the topic and give background information.

A bonsai plant is not naturally small in size. Special techniques are used to make it grow in such a way that it fits into a small container. One common technique is to prune the roots, leaves and branches regularly as the tree grows. A bonsai tree retains all the features and qualities of the full-grown version.

Bonsai trees can be given various artistic shapes by wiring the trunk and branches. While almost any woody plant can be used to create a bonsai, the pine, maple, elm, flowering cherry, silky oak and fig trees are the most popular choices, as their leaves are naturally small.

Body
Develop the topic with detailed information.

Many people like to use bonsai plants for decorating their homes. However, bonsai plants do not survive for long without open air and sunlight. They also have to be watered very carefully as excess water can spoil the roots. Special knowledge and skill is required to take proper care of a bonsai plant.

Conclusion
Make a final comment on the most important point about the topic.

 ISBN 978-93-5103-602-9

Let's Practise

Use the outline to write a report.

Swimming, a Fun Way to Keep Fit

Introduction: popular sport – excellent exercise – has many health benefits – also a great source of fun – suitable for people of all ages – does not cost much

Body: can be risky for beginners – important to learn from an experienced trainer – important to use the correct swimming gear – lots of clubs where swimming is taught – swimming tournaments draw huge crowds

Conclusion: healthy activity that you can do all your life – helps you to relax and feel good – great way to make friends – young people should be encouraged to take up this activity

 ISBN 978-93-5103-602-9

13.2 Story

A story is an account of a real or imaginary event or series of events.

Take Note
A story has three main parts:
1. Beginning
2. Middle
3. Ending

Rescue from the Cliff

"Help!" The shout came from below. Rima and Bobby heard it as they walked up the cliff path. They stopped and looked very cautiously over the edge. About twenty feet down they spotted a boy sitting on a rocky ledge, looking up at them.

Beginning
Make the beginning of a story interesting. Present the problem in the story.

"Hi!" he called. "Can you fetch a rope?"

"Are you hurt?" shouted Bobby.

"My ankle!" he shouted. "It's very sore!"

"Bobby," said Rima, "you stay right here with him, and I'll get help."

There was a farmhouse nearby, and Rima knew the farmer. She ran there as fast as she could. Bobby asked the boy's name.

"I'm Sajid," he called. "I was running along the path when I slipped and slid down, luckily on to this ledge."

Middle
Develop the events in the story.

It wasn't long before Rima came back with the farmer, who was carrying a long rope. He let it down to Sajid.

"Tie it round your waist tightly with a really strong knot," he called.

Sajid managed to do this. Then the farmer pulled the rope up. Sajid reached the top of the cliff, and the farmer drove him with his two new friends to the hospital.

Ending
Show how the problem is resolved.

 ISBN 978-93-5103-602-9

Let's Practise

Use the outline to write a story.

An Adventure in the Forest

Beginning: three children (give their names) taking a walk – a new path into the forest suddenly appears

Middle: they follow it – they come to a strange old house – inside is a table laid with food – the children eat and drink – suddenly everything vanishes – the path is gone – they are lost

Ending: a wolf appears – they follow it out of the forest

 ISBN 978-93-5103-602-9

13.3 Diary

A diary is a notebook where you write about the things that happen to you every day, and your thoughts and feelings. Each day's record is called a diary entry.

Take Note

A diary entry
- is a personal note that describes events, feelings and experiences.
- may leave out words like **I** and **we** to save space and time.
- is usually written in the past tense.

Saturday, 12 March 2016

Dear Diary,

Hurray! The weekend! Got up at 7.30 and ate breakfast (pancakes and honey) with Mum and Dad. Diya and Ayan got up late and we all went into town by bus to go shopping. First into Lal's new department store. Dad and Ayan went to find sports clothes, and Mum, Diya and I looked for swimming costumes for our holiday in Penang. I got a lovely red one. Had lunch in the store's restaurant. I had fruit salad and vanilla pudding. Delicious. Walked to the science museum and saw an engineering exhibition. Lots of fantastic machines to operate! Decided to stay in town and see a film at the Roxy Cinema. It was *Animal Crackers* with the Marx Brothers. Brilliant. Couldn't stop laughing. Home by taxi at nine o'clock. Great day!

What to write

Write things in your diary that will interest you when you read it later on.

 ISBN 978-93-5103-602-9

Let's Practise

Use the outline to write a diary entry.

a school day – fine weather – get up – breakfast – to school (mention form of transport) – lessons (give details) – everything interrupted by fire drill – lunch – gym class – home – homework – relaxed evening (mention details) – surprise special dish at dinner

 ISBN 978-93-5103-602-9

Review 4

1. Read the article and answer the questions below in your notebook.

The First Marathon

As the world prepares for the 2016 Summer Olympics, it is time to look back upon the origins of the Olympic Games. One of the toughest events in the Olympics is the marathon, and this heroic race has a long history.

In 490 BC, the Persian king Darius sent a huge army to attack the Greek city of Athens, because the Athenians had been supporting rebels within the Persian kingdom. Darius's army crossed the Aegean Sea and landed on the island of Euboea, then crossed to Marathon, on the east coast of Greece, about 24 miles (40 kilometres) north-east of Athens. The Athenian army numbered only ten thousand, but the soldiers fought with all their strength and courage and, miraculously, managed to defeat the enormous Persian army. Many Persian soldiers were killed, and the rest fled.

A messenger was chosen to take the news of the victory to Athens. His name was Pheidippides. He ran all the way from Marathon to Athens but, just as he got there and reported the victory, he collapsed with exhaustion and died.

The first Olympic Games of modern times were held in Athens in 1896, and one of the events was a long-distance run from Marathon to Athens, commemorating the non-stop run of Pheidippides all those centuries ago. Since then, the marathon has been a regular Olympic event.

a. What is the main idea of the article?

b. In the brackets, number the sentences in the correct order.

   i. Darius's army landed on the island of Euboea. [ ]

   ii. Darius's army crossed the Aegean Sea. [ ]

   iii. Darius's army crossed to Marathon. [ ]

c. Why was the Battle of Marathon such an amazing Athenian victory?

d. Write a summary of how the marathon got its name.

e. From the article, find the following:

   i. one similarity and one difference between the modern marathon and Pheidippides's run

   ii. a sentence that uses the present perfect tense

   iii. three abstract nouns

f. What does the word **commemorating** mean? Tick the correct answer.

   i. celebrating ii. defeating iii. enjoying

 ISBN 978-93-5103-602-9

2. Read the newspaper report and answer the questions below in your notebook.

Raipur: A massive fire broke out at 10 p.m. last night on the seventh floor of Asiana Apartments on Northern Avenue. A local shopkeeper, Pawan Bansal, noticed the flames and informed the police and the fire station. Fire engines were immediately rushed to the spot and the blaze was doused after more than three hours of firefighting.

One person died and three others suffered severe burns in the incident. The deceased has been identified as Ram Kumar Sharma (35). The injured have been admitted to the Civil Hospital. One of them is in a critical condition.

It is believed that the fire was caused by the explosion of a gas cylinder in Sharma's kitchen. Deputy Superintendent of Police (DSP) Hari Prasad said that investigations are being made into the exact reason for the fire.

a. When and where did the fire break out?

b. How did the police get to know about the fire?

c. What do you think will happen next?

d. Read each statement. In the brackets, write **F** if it is a fact or **O** if it is an opinion.

i. The fire engines were sent to the spot immediately. [ ]

ii. The name of the deceased person was Ram Kumar Sharma. [ ]

iii. The fire was caused by the explosion of a gas cylinder. [ ]

e. Tick the correct answer.

You can conclude that Pawan Bansal was a helpful man because

i. he was a shopkeeper.

ii. he noticed the flames.

iii. he informed the police and the fire station about the fire.

f. In the brackets, number the sentences in the correct order.

i. The injured have been admitted to the Civil Hospital. [ ]

ii. Fire engines were immediately rushed to the spot. [ ]

iii. Investigations are being made into the exact reason for the fire. [ ]

g. What does the word **deceased** mean? Tick the correct answer.

i. struck by a disease ii. dead iii. injured

Spot the Error

h. Circle the error in each sentence. Write the correct word in the blank.

i. A fire broke out on a seventh floor of Asiana Apartments. ____________

ii. The fire was brung under control after three hours. ____________

iii. The blaze was dozed after a long time. ____________

 ISBN 978-93-5103-602-9

3. Use the outline to write a diary entry.

an evening walk in the park – came across a strange man – he wore a cap and odd clothes – asked me about my school and friends – offered me sweets – I was frightened – came home and told Mum and Dad – Dad promised to come along with me to the park next time – watched quiz programme on television – exciting final round – early dinner and bed

ISBN 978-93-5103-602-9

4. Use the outline to write a story.

a family (give names and details) goes to an animal shelter to adopt a pet – first see a talking parrot that is too rude – then see a monkey that is too naughty – then see a rabbit that is too lazy – the children about to give up hope when they see a shy puppy – puppy becomes playful and sweet on being called – family adopt it finally and take it home

 ISBN 978-93-5103-602-9

Word Power

Nouns ending in -sion and -tion

Nouns that end in **-sion** or **-tion** have a similar ending sound.

Fill in the blanks with **-sion** or **-tion**.

1. When you're upset, it's difficult to control your emo _ _ _ _ s.
2. Can you see a connec _ _ _ _ between the two happenings?
3. The sound is okay, but the vi _ _ _ _ has disappeared.
4. One of the most important inven _ _ _ _ s of the twentieth century was the computer.
5. A wedding is a happy occa _ _ _ _.
6. They are building an exten _ _ _ _ to the theatre.

Words that are easily confused

There are some pairs of words that sound similar, but have different spellings and meanings.

Fill in the blanks with the correct words.

1. Doctors ________ us to eat more fruit. We should follow their ________. (advice/advise)
2. Too much rainfall will ________ the farmers directly, because it will have a bad ________ on the crops. (affect/effect)
3. We ________ all your suggestions ________ the last one. (except/accept)
4. When I ________ weight, these trousers will become too ________ for me. (lose/loose)
5. We stayed in a hotel on the edge of the ________. After dinner, we had dates and ice cream for ________. (dessert/desert)
6. Playing an instrument needs a lot of ________, so I try to ________ every day. (practise/practice)

 ISBN 978-93-5103-602-9

Prefixes and suffixes

A prefix is a group of letters that we add to the beginning of a word to make it a new word.

A suffix is a group of letters that we add to the end of a word to make it a new word.

Prefix	Meaning	Examples
anti-	against, or the opposite	**anti**septic, **anti**social
dis-	not, or the opposite	**dis**like, **dis**comfort
mis-	wrongly or badly	**mis**behave, **mis**match
non-	not	**non**-existent, **non**-member
re-	again	**re**write, **re**play
un-	not, or the opposite	**un**kind, **un**dress

Suffix	Meaning	Examples
-**able**	able to be treated some way	solv**able**, drink**able**
-**ful**	full of a quality	wonder**ful**, hope**ful**
-**ish**	slightly, or like	yellow**ish**, fever**ish**
-**less**	without something	use**less**, taste**less**
-**ness**	the quality of something	soft**ness**, rough**ness**

1. Fill in the blanks by adding a prefix to the word(s) given in the brackets.
   a. Please ________________ these sentences. You've made a lot of mistakes. (write)
   b. Dave's ________________ remarks made me ________________. (kind, happy)
   c. You will be punished for your ________________. (behaviour)
   d. I ________________ her because she was ________________. (liked, honest)
   e. Sophie ________________ and got into bed. (dress)

2. Fill in each blank by adding a suffix to the word given in the brackets.
   a. The food was not very nice. It was rather ________________. (taste)
   b. Are you okay? You look a bit ________________. (fever)
   c. Is the water in the stream ________________? (drink)
   d. I'm glad the situation is looking more ________________. (hope)
   e. A blunt knife is quite ________________. (use)

 ISBN 978-93-5103-602-9

Similes and metaphors

Both similes and metaphors are used to make comparisons. They compare a person or thing to something that is known for a certain quality.

A simile uses **as** or **like** for the comparison, for example, I was **as busy as a bee** (very busy) all morning.

A metaphor makes the comparison without using **as** or **like**, for example, That news is **music to my ears** (wonderful to hear).

1. Look at each sentence. Tick the correct box to indicate if it contains a simile or a metaphor.

	Simile	Metaphor
a. Rana can swim like a fish.	☐	☐
b. You are asking for the moon.	☐	☐
c. David ran like the wind.	☐	☐
d. It's raining cats and dogs.	☐	☐
e. He's such a baby when it comes to getting an injection.	☐	☐
f. I was as warm as toast in my bed.	☐	☐
g. They just seemed to be talking hot air.	☐	☐
h. Mina and Nina are as alike as two peas in a pod.	☐	☐

2. Similes often refer to certain animals that are well known for a particular quality. Choose an animal from the box to complete each simile.

lion	mule	fox	peacock	owl	lamb	mouse	eel	ox

Example as strong as an ox

a. as gentle as a ______________
b. as proud as a ______________
c. as wise as an ______________
d. as quiet as a ______________
e. as slippery as an ______________
f. as cunning as a ______________
g. as brave as a ______________
h. as stubborn as a ______________

 ISBN 978-93-5103-602-9

Words that go together

There are certain words that are almost always used together. For example, we say we **shake** somone's **hand** when we grip somone's hand in greeting. Similarly, we **key** a **message** or a **password** when we are using our computer.

1. Circle the word that fits each sentence.

Example We are (changing / moving) house next week.

a. Sam was sleeping (soundly / hard).

b. We visited the (ruined / broken) fort.

c. You (said / told) a lie.

d. The traffic was held up by a (still / stationary) vehicle.

e. I (kept / held) my promise.

f. Harry was (badly / severely) punished.

g. The top of the mountain was (clearly / brightly) visible.

h. Anna was (rewarded / awarded) a prize.

i. The wicked witch had vanished without a (sign / trace).

j. Make sure the lids of the jars fit (closely / tightly).

2. Fill in each blank with the correct verb from the box below.

do	have	take	give	make

a. I never get time to __________ my hair properly.

b. Would you __________ a photo of us, please?

c. We shall have to __________ the car a push.

d. I'd better __________ the beds.

e. Let's __________ a party!

3. Fill in each blank with the correct preposition from the box below.

in	on	by	at	under	with

a. We're performing a play __________ Shakespeare.

b. Children __________ five travel free.

c. The twins are always fighting __________ each other.

d. You look very pretty __________ this photo.

e. I know I can always depend __________ you.

f. Mr Bose is good __________ taking charge.

ISBN 978-93-5103-602-9